CONSULTING WITH HUMAN SERVICE SYSTEMS

CONSULTING WITH HUMAN SERVICE SYSTEMS

Leonard D. Goodstein
Arizona State University

 **ADDISON-WESLEY
PUBLISHING COMPANY**

Reading, Massachusetts
Menlo Park, California
London • Amsterdam
Don Mills, Ontario • Sydney

This book is in the
ADDISON-WESLEY SERIES IN
CLINICAL AND PROFESSIONAL
PSYCHOLOGY

Leonard D. Goodstein
Series Editor

To My Parents

Foreword

Clinical psychology is a rapidly expanding area of inquiry and practice. Traditional lines between clinical and the other subdisciplines of psychology are rapidly eroding. Research in information processing has direct impact upon behavior therapy, work in physiological psychology affects our work in biofeedback, community psychologists need to keep abreast of what is happening in social psychology, and so on. At the same time, clinical psychologists are being called on to work in a variety of new settings, and to continually develop new skills as well as to utilize their existing skills. Health Maintenance organizations (HMOs) ask clinical psychologists not only to provide direct clinical service to clients but also to help change the health-related behaviors of clients who do not require direct service.

Community mental health centers ask their clinicians to provide direct service and to assist in developing prevention programs and program evaluation procedures. These are but a few examples of how the field of clinical psychology is expanding.

It is difficult for the professional practitioner as well as the student of clinical psychology to keep in touch with what is happening in the field. Traditional textbooks can give only superficial coverage to these recent changes and the journal literature does not provide a broad overview. The Addison-Wesley Series in Clinical and Professional Psychology is an effort to fill this gap. Taken as a whole, the series could be used as an introduction to the field of clinical psychology. A subset of these books, such as those on therapy, for example, could serve as a text for a course in therapy. Single volumes can be used for seminars when supplemented by journal articles, or as supplemental texts for courses in which the instructor feels the text is lacking in coverage of that area, or for short courses for the active professional. We hope that each of these volumes, written or edited by experts in the area, will also serve as an up-to-date overview of that area for the interested professional who feels in the need of updating.

In this volume the author has attempted to provide an introduction to the rapidly developing field of organizational consultation. Beginning with an overview of the concepts and approaches to organizational consultation, the volume reviews the steps involved in such consultation and other kinds of interventions.

Webster defines a *primer* as "a small introductory volume on a subject." It is hoped that this volume will serve such a function in the area of organizational consultation.

Leonard D. Goodstein

Preface

Organizational consultation is an important and rapidly growing field of professional activity. Most of the published literature on the subject, however, deals with the private or profit-making sector. The organizational consultant and those interested in becoming consultants to public or nonprofit organizations have had to rely either upon the incomplete literature on working in the nonprofit area or upon the literature about profit-making organizations. Such a reliance can be problematic as there are a number of important differences between nonprofit and profit-making organizations, differences which have major consequences for those consultants who wish to be successful with either of these kinds of organizations. It is hoped that the present volume will be useful in relieving this problem.

There are many clinical psychologists and other mental health professionals who will question their own interest in this area. They typically argue that they are interested in direct client service and have little or no interest in consulting with organizations. Without suggesting any changes in their career focuses, however, there is much in this book which should be of interest to such professionals. Many of them work, or have worked, in human service delivery systems and their effectiveness as clinicians is directly affected by the organizational characteristics of those systems. Further, almost all of us and our families have routine, sometimes daily, contact with these human service delivery systems—schools, churches, hospital and other health care facilities, parks, governmental agencies, and so on. A better understanding of the organizational issues involved in such agencies should be helpful both in being a more informed consumer and in supporting the kinds of changes that are required for such organizations to meet more effectively the needs of our society.

This book is presumably useful for courses in consultation methods, organizational psychology, community psychology, and organizational development. It should also be useful for professional consultants who are often perplexed by the special difficulties they encounter when they attempt to work with public-sector agencies.

The volume is easily divided into two major sections, the first four chapters are an overview of the conceptual issues involved in understanding organizations and the consultation process while the last four chapters involve a sequential analysis of what happens in providing organization consultation. More specifically, Chapter 1 highlights some of the ways that human service delivery systems differ from business and industrial organizations. The second chapter comprises three major theoretical analyses of consultation. Chapter 3 is an analysis of process consultation, the mode recommended throughout this work, while Chapter 4 is a brief overview of organizational theory, especially as it illuminates human service organizations.

While the last four chapters deal with the stages or phases of organizational consultation, we want to underscore that these neat, clean blocks exist only in textbooks of consultation and are convenient abstractions for didactic purposes. With that caveat, the last four chapters deal with entry issues or beginning the consultation

(Chapter 5), the centrality of diagnosis in consultation (Chapter 6), the various interventions that are possible in organizational consultation (Chapter 7), and the final stages of evaluating and terminating the consulting relationship (Chapter 8).

A number of people have been specially helpful in bringing this book to completion. Jeanette Treat Goodstein was, as always, my strongest supporter and my severest critic. John Crosby, Jr., my colleague and friend, read the entire manuscript and made a number of important suggestions. Two other friends and colleagues, W. Warner Burke and Marvin Weisbord, not only have read portions of the manuscript and provided helpful feedback but, more importantly, have been continually part of my personal and professional support system while I was developing many of these ideas. Finally, but equally importantly, Mary Redondo and Helen Rubio have provided expert and uncomplaining secretarial help during the writing and editing of the entire project.

Tempe, Arizona   L. D. G.
November 1977

Acknowledgments

The author gratefully acknowledges the permission to reproduce materials previously published:

Addison-Wesley Publishing Company to reproduce "Characteristics of unhealthy and healthy organizations" from J. K. Fordyce and R. Weil's *Managing with People.* Reading, Mass.: Addison-Wesley, 1971, pp. 11–14.

Marvin R. Weisbord and Organization Research and Development to reproduce "The six-box model," from M. Weisbord's "Organizational diagnosis: Six places to look for trouble with or without a theory." *Group and Organization Studies* (1976) *1*, 430–447.

Robert R. Blake and Jane Srygley Mouton to reproduce the Consulcube T. M. from R. R. Blake and J. S. Mouton's *Consultation.* Reading, Mass.: Addison-Wesley, 1976, page 7.

Contents

1

Organizational Issues in Human Service Delivery Systems

Process Versus Product Concerns   1

Human Service Delivery Systems   5

The Public Sector   7

The Third Sector   14

2

Understanding the Consultation Process

Background of Understanding   18

Mental Health Consultation   23

The Consulcube   28

3

Dimensions of Process Consultation

Process Versus Content Concerns   39

Value Issues in Organizational Consultation   46

Process Consultation and Other Models of Consultation   55

4

Some Approaches to Understanding Organizations

Need for Understanding Organizations   58

An Open-Systems Approach to Understanding Organizations   60

The Tavistock Institute and Psychoanalytic Approaches   64

The Consulcube   66

Process Consultation Approaches
to Understanding Organizations   69

A Differentiation-Integration Model
for Understanding Organizations   72

Weisbord's Six-Box Model
of Understanding Organizations   74

5

Entry Issues in Organizational Consultation

The Initial Contact   77

The Contract   86

Value Dilemmas in Consultation   90

6

Diagnosis in Consultation

Resistance to Diagnosis   96

Methods of Data Collection   98

The Inquiry Process   101

The Six Boxes Revisited   103
The Role of Diagnosis   113

7

Interventions in Consultation

Diagnosis as Part of Intervention   116
Planning the Intervention   119
A Typology of Organizational Interventions   122
Technostructural Interventions   124
Process Interventions   133

8

Later Stages in Consultation

Criteria to Judge Change   142
Terminating a Consulting Relationship   149
Roles Consultants Play   150
Consultants as Marginal Employees   155
Evaluating Consultation   157

References   163
Index   168

Organizational Issues in Human Service Delivery Systems

Process Versus Product Concerns

The Lakeside Plant of the Acme Motor Car Company has long been regarded as one of the trouble spots in the Acme organization. Managers who are sent there from other plants regard themselves as having been "sent to Siberia." Housed in a dilapidated World War II plant that was built for another purpose, the transmissions built there cost more to produce than at other plants. There is a very high scrappage rate, high product costs, especially in comparison with other plants, and a low yield on investment. Industrial sabotage is rampant and worker morale is low, as evidenced by a high absentee rate and the highest utilization of sick leave in the entire Acme organization.

The Health Department of River City, often called the "Graveyard of Health Commissioners," is now testing its fourth incumbent in six years. Meetings of the Board of Health, the organization responsible for managing the department, are frequently disrupted either by groups of dissident workers who demand better working conditions or by citizens who demand higher-quality health care. The commissioner's plan to reorganize the Department cannot be implemented because of resistance by the old-time middle managers in the department. Staff meetings drag on endlessly with little being accomplished, and staff turnover, especially among the younger personnel recruited by the most recent commissioner, is high.

These two brief case histories clearly suggest that organizations can find themselves experiencing difficulties, just as do individuals, families, and other collections of people. These difficulties can be evidenced in a variety of ways. They include overt conflict between organizational members or between segments of the society; failure of the organization to attract or retain members; frequent absences from organizational work; inability of members of the organization to agree upon the primary task of the organization or to agree upon the priority of goals; and so on. All of these organizational difficulties involve *process* concerns. By process concerns we mean those factors, primarily interperson or intergroup, which are involved in how the organization goes about doing its work.

These process concerns stand in contrast to *product* concerns. By product concerns we mean those more impersonal factors, such as raw materials, machinery, plants or offices, etc. that are involved in producing the goods or services the organization is attempting to provide. In other words, product refers to the goods or services which the organization produces—the *what* of the organization—while process refers to *how* the organization goes about producing those products or services, especially how it organizes its human resources.

The distinction between process and product is perhaps clearest in the business and industrial sector. There raw materials are obtained, are changed in some rather clear-cut and accepted fashion into a new product, and are then shipped out. Product concerns, of course, are affected by process concerns—by the way the people are organized, how the plant is laid out, how decisions are made, how well the organization meets the personal needs of the people who work there, and so on—but more about these in a moment.

A business or industrial organization may be less effective because of its inability to handle product concerns. It may need help on designing a more effective machine to produce its product, or it may require greater capital for expansion, or access to new markets. For help with these product concerns, organizations turn to technical, product-oriented specialists, and to consultants from engineering, finance, and marketing.

But when an organization experiences process concerns of the sort described above, concerns involving human resources, the organization may turn to an organizational consultant. Psychologists, because of their training in listening to and understanding people, have been extensively used to help organizations resolve these process concerns. We shall explore this process of organizational consultation in more detail.

Before we proceed, however, it should be noted that the distinction between product and process becomes less clear as we move from business and industrial organizations to public service ones. These organizations in the public sector, both governmental and community based, typically offer some kind of human service—education, public safety, welfare, health, or the like. Since there is no finished product in any tangible sense as there is in a factory to serve as buffer between the internal processes of the organization and what is offered to the public, the internal processes of human service delivery systems are more obvious, more exposed to the final consumer. While a purchaser of a new car may assume that the failure to install the transmission adequately is the result of some failure of communication within the automobile factory, the helpless patient who is sent from desk to desk in an outpatient section of a large hospital can see the communication failures directly unfold before his or her own eyes. In human service delivery systems the process is the product delivered at the end point to the final consumer.

We shall concentrate our attention on these human service delivery systems, both those organizations in the public sector and those voluntary or nonprofit organizations which stand at the interface of the private and public sectors, the so-called third sector (Levitt, 1973).*

Public sector organizations are those federal, state, and local organizations such as city and county health departments, public schools, public welfare departments, departments of public safety (police and fire services), correctional institutions, federal veterans programs, including veterans hospitals, the Peace Corps and VISTA, and the federal social security system. Third sector organizations are those which are neither private nor public but which attempt "to do things business or government are either not doing, not doing well, or not doing often enough" (Levitt, 1973, p. 49). A wide range of organizations are typically a part of the third sector category, such as hospitals and health organizations, including mental health; social service agencies, including family planning, welfare, and consumer organizations; cultural agencies, such as symphony orchestras, little theatre groups, zoos and museums, churches, political parties, unions and fraternal organizations, independent colleges and universities; and private foundations and other fund-raising organizations, such as the March of Dimes, the

---

*Further details on references can be found in the References at the back of the book.

American Cancer Society, and so on. All of these organizations, both public and those in the third sector, deliver some kind of human service rather than a tangible product, and thus share in revealing their internal processes through their service delivery.

Human Service Delivery Systems

Although organizations engaged in human service delivery are ubiquitous and involve a substantial portion of the total work force, little has been written on their special qualities. Most of the books on organizational consultation, for example, have concentrated their attention on organizations in the private, profit-making sector, except for a few that have focused on public schools (Sarason, Levine, Goldenberg, Cherlin, and Bennett, 1966; Schmuck and Miles, 1971).

There are a number of reasons for us to concern ourselves with organizational consultation in these human services organizations. Not the least of these is that psychologists themselves are more likely to be employed by such organizations than by business or industrial organizations. The presence of such psychologists not only initially gives the work of organizational consultants more credibility but also these internal personnel can serve as resources in the developing consultation.

Further, psychologists are often contacted by human services organizations as technical specialists to help the organization with specific issues before any more general process concerns are ever raised. Thus, psychologists can be asked by a police department for help with their psychological screening procedures, or by a social service agency to help draft a research proposal to evaluate an experimental program with alcoholics, or by a school to review its human-relations training curriculum. As the psychologist successfully addresses these technical issues over time, more general process issues about the organization and how it goes about doing its work may be raised. The police raise questions about how their relations with the black community can be improved, the social service agency becomes interested in more generally evaluating the impact of their functioning, and the school begins to question how administrative staff, teachers, and pupils can work more effectively together.

So we see that a technical consultation can evolve into a more general organizational process consultation and, for psychologists, this kind of transformation is much more possible in a human services delivery system than in a plant or factory. Such a change is possible because the psychologist can more readily gain internal access into the human service delivery system. This access is a result of his or her perceived expertise in such systems, an expertise most psychologists, particularly those trained in a more classical tradition, do not have in the private sector.

There is, however, an even more important reason for our interest in human service delivery systems. It is to such systems that troubled persons of all sorts turn for help—the emotionally disturbed, the retarded, the handicapped, and the impoverished. Those of us concerned with alleviating such human problems must recognize that the systems through which help is to be delivered must be readily accessible, technically competent, and responsive to demands if there is to be any alleviation of human misery. Clearly it is not enough to develop new theories or techniques of counseling or therapy, new procedures of rehabilitation or whatever, if the system in which they are intended to function is incapable of using them. Only recently have mental health professionals become aware of the importance of the overall social system through which their expertise is marketed to society. Organizational consultation is one effort by these professionals to improve the human condition by effecting change in the total delivery system rather than by simply changing the manner in which the professional deals directly with troubled people.

There are also several intrinsic, substantive reasons for concentrating our attention on human service delivery systems, as they are indeed different from organizations in the private sector. Two of these differences should be apparent in our brief case studies presented at the beginning of this chapter. The description of the Lakeside Plant of Acme Motors offers several instances of the direct financial cost of the organizational malaise at Lakeside. The year-end profit-and-loss statement for the plant will show it to be an unprofitable enterprise for the corporation. While the corporation's overall financial picture might be profitable and, thus, there may be reasons for not closing down the Lakeside plant, this alternative will certainly be considered. In the private sector no organization can long exist in an unprofitable state. Success is clearly measurable as profit, although other considerations always enter into evaluations as well.

In the public and third sectors, however, there is no such clear criterion of success. How does one measure the success of a public school, a community mental-health center, a public library, a fire department, or any other public-service organization? Since such organizations are not profit oriented, no measure of profit can be used. While cost effectiveness and accountability of such human service delivery systems have long been proposed, it should be clear that there is no commonly accepted, single yardstick for evaluating these agencies. Furthermore, human service delivery systems rarely go out of business.

The Public Sector

While there are some similarities between public and third sector organizations—the most important of which is that there rarely tends to be a tangible product involved—there are a number of important differences. Indeed, many organizational theorists, such as Levitt (1973), decry the failure of organizational researchers to study these differences. Let us first examine some of the special characteristics of public agencies before we return to our examination of the third sector.

In order to improve organizational effectiveness, the sociologist Max Weber (1947) proposed that all organizations operate in a highly logical and impersonal fashion. Such a rational organization he termed a *bureaucracy*, and its main virtues were its cold, logical approach and the exclusion of emotional or nonrational considerations from its operations. Human beings who worked in such organizations could readily be substituted for one another—as spare parts—and the basic underlying value of such organizations was to operate in accordance with the logical and carefully prescribed procedures. Weber regarded bureaucracy as technically superior to any other form of organization because of its rationality, efficiency, and competence.

Today bureaucracy has come to mean organizational waste and inefficiency, especially in the public sector. Why? Apparently, the private sector—with its emphasis on task accomplishment and consequent profit—does not reward those who follow "proper procedures," "clearing it through channels," and so on. Rather, rewards and promotions are more likely to accrue to the innovative and task-oriented individual who finds a way to get the job done, although the informal organizational norms are almost always followed. It is primarily in the public sector, with its innumerable volumes of rules and regulations—where success is evaluated by whether or not the rules and regulations have been obeyed rather than by task accomplishment—that bureaucracy has flourished. It can be noted in this connection that many very large and noncompetitive organizations in the private sector—public utilities, for example—tend to be as bureaucratic in their organizational life as those in the public sector.

The major point of this digression, however, is that many organizations in the public sector are ordinarily not task oriented but rather are bureaucratic, especially well-established "old-line" agencies. This means that doing things properly is more important than getting things done—an approach which can best be maintained in organizations without a profit motive. As Eddy and Saunders (1972) note, most governmental organizations were built upon and still conform to this traditional bureaucratic model. The focus is on efficiency and rationality, a pyramidal (hierarchical) authority system, a differentiation of tasks into separate bureaus, sections, or offices, and an explicit system of rules and regulations to control the behavior of all who work there.

A second characteristic of public sector organizations, implicit in our examples, is that persons who need these human care systems have no alternative source for that service; typically there are no competitors. Children are sent to the public schools in "their" district, one calls the local police or fire department, the indigent go to the local public out-patient clinics, and so on. These citizens either accept the services as offered by these institutions or they do without. While there are occasional exceptions to this statement, such as private schools, free clinics, and so on, they are rare. The absence of competition from other service purveyors makes most human service delivery systems quite complacent about themselves and the services they offer. They are guaranteed a potential clientele based upon estimates of the population in their district who need their particular service; they are funded on the basis of these estimates, estimates which they frequently make themselves, and they are left free of many requirements that they demonstrate effectiveness.

But, at the same time, public sector organizations are subject to diverse pressures at many levels, what Golembiewski (1969) terms "multiple access to multiple authoritative decision makers" (p. 370). By this he means that public sector organizations are both responsible to, and responsive to, not only the executive branch of government in which they are embedded, but also the legislative branch which creates and funds them. Further, such public agencies are influenced by a variety of "special interest groups" such as professional associations of teachers, physicians, and others, consumer groups, regulatory commissions, and so on. Lastly, the mass media carefully monitor much of what is done in the public sector, determined to expose and rout out bureaucratic incompetence and the like. All of these pressures suggest that public business is viewed from a variety of different perspectives and must be responsive, to a greater or lesser degree, to each of these. In contrast, business and industrial organizations operate much more privately and do not need to be as responsive to such pressures. These pressures tend to make public agencies cautious and fearful of innovation, lest they be chastized for being wasteful and lacking in proper concern for the public good. Further, there is a strong norm of "covering your ass" in order to prevent being identified as responsible for any such failures in such public agencies. Such a norm makes it difficult to identify how any decision is made or implemented.

One further characteristic of public agencies is that the top level of management tends to be filled by political appointment rather than by career service personnel. This limits the positions to which career public employees can aspire and further means that the top level of management in the public sector is more concerned with politics, with reappointment as its primary concern rather than the proper management of the agency. Also, this system gives rise to rapid and dramatic changes in the top-level management, even though these changes occur on a fairly regular time sequence.

There are a number of other patterns and behaviors that tend to typify public agencies, namely, the "habit backgrounds" initially suggested by Golembiewski (1969). In public agencies, managers at all levels are reluctant to delegate authority but rather tend to maximize information and control at the uppermost levels, presumably where the responsibility is set by legislative mandate. This "layering" of multiple levels of review tends to centralize power in public agencies and to decrease innovation and self-direction anywhere in the agency.

Second, there are legal and legalistic specifications of appropriate and inappropriate work behaviors. In government agencies, roles are much more clearly defined than in the private sector and there is greater reluctance to move out of what has been specifically defined as one's appropriate role. Who has not been infuriated by waiting in a line at one window of the post office or other governmental agency while the other windows, all with clerks apparently unoccupied, have been unable or unwilling to answer our questions, sell us stamps, deliver a registered letter, or whatever?

A third characteristic on Golembiewski's list is a strong need for security. While military and defense agencies can argue that they indeed have a need for keeping their work out of the public domain, the need for security has extended into all areas of government. The recent rise in the so-called sunshine laws requiring government agencies to conduct their decision making in public can be seen as a reaction to what has been regarded as excessive secrecy in government. At the same time, however, it should be noted that business and industrial organizations are probably even more secretive in going about their business, yet their unwillingness to open their operations to public scrutiny is not regarded with the same concern. Clearly this paradox reflects our previous point that the public's business is seen as everyone's concern and the media feel that they have a mandate to report on the actions of government agencies. The need for secrecy in government agencies may be seen as one attempt to limit the pressure from the media and other sources, especially early in the making of decisions.

A fourth characteristic is the tendency for government agencies to stress procedural regularity and caution. Accountability can be seen as the watchword for many governmental agencies. In practice, however, this tends to mean a blizzard of paperwork, a profusion of signatures and countersignatures, and an unwillingness to be seen as the individual responsible for having made a decision.

The fifth and last of Golembiewski's habit backgrounds is that the concept of the professional manager is less well developed in the public sector than in the private. In the private sector managers are brought in from outside the organization with great regularity, selected primarily for their proven managerial competence. In the public sector, however, managers are promoted from within, selected from civil service lists which place heavy emphasis on seniority within the organization, and there is little trust placed in the concept of the "public professional manager." Those professional managers who do exist tend to find themselves frequently at odds with their superiors, the elected public officials, about who has the "right" to make certain decisions and to whom the professional manager owes his or her expertise, while the elected official resents the fact that the professional manager has not stood for public office. In this connection, it can be noted that the salaries for top-level managers in the public sector are significantly lower than those in the private sector. As one example of this, and a hint of the underlying reasons, we can note that the Congress has mandated that no Civil Service employee of the United States government can be paid more than a United States Congressman.

While these five habit backgrounds are far from a complete list, they do suggest that there are a number of important differences between public and private institutions. One important reason for our attention to these psychological issues is that organizational consultants in the public sector need to be aware of the differences and understand that they are naturally occurring phenomena. Further, the differences not only limit the range of changes which might be considered, but also clearly set a rather different timetable for the creation of change in the public sector, and require different methods for accomplishment.

One additional point needs to be made before we move from this discussion of the public sector. Most of the special characteristics of public agencies are well known, to a greater or lesser degree, to most intelligent and well-educated persons. Given that most of the comparisons between public and private agencies tend to give the public ones a negative image, what does that mean about the many men and women who choose careers in government service, especially those who aspire to management careers in the public sector?

It is indeed unfortunate that we have no research-based data upon which to answer this question. Rather, we must rely upon our own informal observations and prevailing stereotypes about government workers. Clearly, government service must be regarded as attractive to individuals who prefer certainty and security to ambiguity and conflict. Most students of organizational life believe that people choose to work in organizations that tend to meet their personal needs (e. g., Harrison, 1972) and that there are personnel turnover and conflict when this does not occur. What this means for government service is that a large percentage of such employees find comfort in not being involved in making decisions, in having their roles carefully specified and limited, in working cautiously under procedural controls, and in having limited and carefully specified career development ladders. Such people are clearly different from those who choose the more competitive, ambiguous, and risky life of the private sector. Nevertheless, it should be clear that we are discussing group differences and that there will be many exceptions to these characterizations.

One of the implications of the differences between people in the private and public sectors involves the management of conflict in these organizations. As we noted earlier, one important consideration of the bureaucratic model is the commitment to rationality. Since conflict can involve emotional elements (indeed strong emotions typify strong conflict, and emotions are nonrational), there should be little open conflict in governmental organizations. Rather conflict should be "smoothed over" with differences compromised away, and direct confrontation between individuals or segments of the organization should be avoided in public sector agencies. Our own experience in interviewing managers in both the public and private sector and in observing a large number of staff meetings in both areas tends to strongly confirm this impression. As one school executive once suggested, "We never argue here. We much prefer the stiletto or the poison cup."

The organizational consultant* working in the public sector will find an open examination of differences between persons and groups to be difficult, especially in contrast to how this is done in the private sector. Important differences will be dismissed, smoothed over, or even denied, especially when an outsider—someone not part of the organizational family—is around to observe and question these differences. We shall return later to a discussion of how some of these differences can be processed more directly, in the interest of organizational vitality.

The Third Sector

Let us now turn our attention to the third sector agencies, those which are neither public nor private. These agencies have been performing various societal functions for many centuries but have increased dramatically in number, size, and scope in the past several decades as we have become more concerned with the nature of our society, its failures, and the inability of both the public and private sectors to deal effectively with social problems. The development of such third sector institutions as Nader's Raiders, the several environmental protection groups like the Sierra Club and Friends of the Earth, health delivery systems like Planned Parenthood and the free clinics are but a few illustrations of this trend.

Many of the characteristics of the public sector organizations discussed above also describe organizations in the third sector. They tend to be service deliverers rather than product producers, especially of human services, and there are no clear criteria of or-

---

*Throughout the book we will refer to consultants in the singular. While we recognize that there are pairs, teams, and other multiples, most organizational consultants do operate alone. We return to this issue in Chapter 8.

ganizational effectiveness. But there are some special aspects of these third sector agencies that should be noted.

Third sector organizations, according to Levitt (1973), are characterized by a focal concern with the redress of social inequities. Levitt further notes that the new third sector organizations, those developed out of the unrest of the 1960's and the war against poverty, not only seek such redress but go even further, aiming at reform, if not revolution, of the social institutions that spawned these inequities. The social-action-oriented new third sector organizations have been more or less successful in establishing more corporate responsibility toward social issues, prison reform, women's and minority rights, and so on; but Levitt notes (1973, p. 103), "The dilemma for America is that the New Third Sector tactics, which seem best able to produce a more responsive and benign society, may also produce a more unstable and malignant society." He goes on to ask how such agencies can continue to prod both public and private institutions into being more responsive without destroying them and the society in which they exist in the process.

Yet another dilemma is pointed out by Merrill (1957) who notes the marginality of such third sector institutions (voluntary associations) and, at the same time, their roles as agents for social change. Thus, for example, specialists in city planning, family relations, and child welfare are all regarded as low-status and low-power persons (especially in contrast with corporation executives and politicians), yet they are seen as doing the important work of society. This paradox leads to many of the frustrations and problems experienced by persons who work in third sector institutions, especially the old ones, and may help explain the rise of the new third sector with its tactics of direct confrontation and political pressure.

Another important difference between third sector organizations on the one hand and private and public organizations on the other is the ambiguity of goals of the third sector (McGill and Wooton, 1975). While private sector organizations have profit as their primary goal and public sector organizations have rationally derived, bureaucratic goals, third sector agencies tend to have general directions or "thrusts," leading to ambiguous and often incompatible or contradictory goals. Levitt's comments on the dilemma faced by the new third sector organizations trying to reform without destroying is but one example. Generally speaking, the third sector organizations have "doing good" broadly defined as their goal, leaving much to the operating managers to define in which "good" and by what strategies the "good" is to be accomplished. In carrying out such a poorly defined set of goals, decisions will frequently be made on a political basis and political influence will be exerted by both members and nonmembers of the organization. The frequent public disputes and staff turmoil in such third sector organizations as the Sierra Club, several of Ralph Nader's public surveillance agencies illustrate this point rather clearly.

In order to achieve the kind of social responsiveness that led to their creation, third sector organizations often attempt to develop management systems of a highly flexible type, using temporary project groups, collegial management, collective leadership, and so on. In order to avoid being guilty of unresponsiveness to social issues, the management system developed in many third sector organizations tends to be poorly structured, often nonrational, and clearly nonhierarchical. But this leads to difficulties in decision making and, frequently, in clearly describing the decision-making process in such organizations; decisions are not "made," they emerge.

There is also a fairly diffuse base of power in such agencies. While this is especially true of the new third sector institutions, it is generally true of virtually all the agencies in the third sector. The relationship between the lay board of directors and the professional staff, between the professional staff and the volunteer staff (volunteer workers are one of the hallmarks of third sector institutions), and between the various professions represented on the professional staff is unclear and frequently marked by covert strife. Further, while these third sector agencies compete in American society for the same prizes as business organizations, namely power, prestige, and money, these goals are never clearly articulated in the same way.

Most students of third sector organizations see these agencies as clearly different from both public and private institutions in terms of their purposes, functions, and characteristics. While there is an enormous range of third sector agencies and important distinctions among them, one can conclude that these institutions may be more flexible, more innovative, and more independent, and are certainly more problematic, than the other two forms of institutions. These are differences that quickly become apparent to the organizational consultant working in the third sector.

Understanding the Consultation Process

Background of Understanding

While there are probably few who would argue that there are many organizations in difficulty and in need of professional help, there are many who would question the adequacy of clinically trained persons for the role of organizational consultant. The typical arguments are that there is little in clinical training that provides any understanding about the social psychology of organizational life, at least not in any formal fashion. Also, clinical training tends to focus the attention of the clinician on the individual rather than on the group or organization, the setting, or other external parameters. And clinically trained persons tend to be preoccupied with the psychopathology of the people they encounter rather than with their strengths or potentials.

To the extent that these stereotypes are true, we have identified limitations in our educational and training programs that require attention. People, both healthy and emotionally disturbed, tend to spend most of their waking hours in organizations and these organizations have enormous impact on people's behavior. Indeed, the work of Stanton and Schwartz (1954) in describing the impact of the social psychology of the mental hospital on both patients and professional staff strongly suggests that no professional clinicians can ignore such organizational issues and how they effect the behavior of all of us. Professionals in the mental health field need a good level of understanding of organizational behavior, particularly those human service delivery systems in which they spend a substantial portion of their professional time. Hopefully, this volume will be a resource in developing that understanding.

The successful organizational consultant needs to bring a variety of skills and knowledge to bear in his or her consultations. These skills involve the ability to diagnose accurately problems of an organizational nature, including both structural and interpersonal ones. The typical organizational consultant, mainly trained in a school of business administration and typically having a business management rather than a clinical background, has a high level of understanding of organizational structures and how they operate, but tends to have less understanding of interpersonal dynamics. The reverse is generally true of those organizational consultants coming from a clinical background. In this case, the clinician is much clearer about the role of interpersonal, and intrapersonal, issues in the organization, yet may overlook or underemphasize the role of structural issues such as reporting lines, communication channels, and so on. It should be clear in both of these instances that we are identifying weaknesses and limitations in the education and background of the organizational consultant, but these limitations require prompt attention if a high level of success is to be attained.

The organizational consultant must also have an understanding of and skill in the consultative process so that he or she is perceived as a "friendly helper" who is nonthreatening, nonjudgmental, and willing to listen. These skills are so much the same as those involved in counseling and therapy, both individual and group, that little more needs to be said about the similarity at this point. Despite the similarity in basic skills, organizational consultation is distinctly different from counseling and therapy. We shall highlight these differences as we continue.

At this juncture it would seem appropriate to point out that one of the potentially unique contributions of the clinically oriented organizational consultant is his or her high-level understanding of personality dynamics and how these dynamics affect behavior, including organizational behavior. Involved here would be an understanding of how special systems of dynamics, needs, motives, and so on can produce personally maladaptive behavior with serious organizational consequences. In one of our own organizational consultations, that with a job-retraining center (Goodstein, 1972), it became clear that one of the principal reasons that internal communications had broken down was because of the seriously disruptive, clinically diagnosable paranoid behavior of one of the key administrative staff. There was a monumental backlog of internal memos, purchase orders, and other administrative work that simply had piled up on his desk while he attempted, unsuccessfully, to determine what was the "hidden meaning" of the documents.

By this example we are not suggesting that human service delivery systems are more likely to attract or retain seriously emotionally disturbed personnel than other types of organizations. Instead, we are suggesting that psychopathology is found in a variety of settings and that the work environment can be seriously affected by an emotionally disturbed person, especially if that person is in a key role in the organization.

A second, less obvious example from the private sector may be helpful in elaborating the point. The young president of a family-owned business asked for an organizational consultation as the result of a successful experience in a sensitivity-training group for managers. It quickly became apparent that he was operating the company in a somewhat reckless fashion, overextending the capacity of the organization to produce and grow. The advice of the other corporate officers was not heeded and morale in the organization, especially among the other officers, was quite low.

Initially it was difficult to determine why this apparently very competent and well-trained executive was behaving in such a poor fashion. Through careful clinical interviews, however, it was revealed that he had taken over the company shortly after his father's death, against the protests of his mother who saw him as too immature for the role. He had promised himself, upon taking over the company, that he would double the net worth of the organization within 18 months, "to prove to Mother that I'm as much a man as my father ever was!" When the organizational consultants began to inquire about the wisdom of some of his actions, especially his unwillingness to deal directly with the rest of the corporate staff, he became outraged at the consultants and accused them of "trying to run my business." The consultation was terminated at this time and, less than a year later, the financial pages of the newspapers reported the bankruptcy of the firm.

These two brief examples suggest the ubiquity of psychopathology in organizational life and the seriousness of its implications. One conclusion that we extract from these data is that an understanding of psychodynamics, including psychopathology, needs to be part of the training of all organizational consultants and that the awareness of psychodynamics issues is one of the unique contributions of the clinically trained organizational consultant.

At the same time it needs to be underscored that there are other considerations that do require attention in organizational consultation. To return again to the job retraining center in our first example, there were a variety of other problematic issues involved in this center that required our attention. For instance, there were two separate bureaucracies, one city and one state, involved in the actual staffing of the agency. The employees of each regarded the other group with apprehension and suspicion, each group believing that it could "do it alone."

The structure of the organization required that workers in each of the separate bureaucracies communicate with each other only "through channels," which meant that, rather than talking directly with the worker at the next desk, a formal memo had to be sent to the top of one hierarchy to one codirector, across to the other codirector, and then down to the other worker. Often the client who was the subject of the memo had quit the program in disgust while waiting for the communication channels to become unclogged. This brief description suggests that there were important structural organizational issues—poor channels of communication, diffuse power, and poor task differentiation—and equally important social and psychological organizational issues—distrust, hostility, and low cooperation—that characterized the organization. While the paranoid staff worker obviously further slowed down an unwieldy communications process, there were other, perhaps even more important organizational matters, both structural and psychological, that lay at the root of the organization's malaise. Again, we stress that the organizational consultant requires a high level of understanding of both organizational structure and organizational dynamics, in addition to psychodynamics, in order to understand how organizations operate.

While we shall continually return to matters of organizational behavior in the course of this volume, it is beyond our scope to provide an in-depth survey of current thinking and research in the social psychology of organizations. The interested reader is referred to Katz and Kahn's (1966) *Social Psychology of Organizations* as one classic text in this area.

Mental Health Consultation

Consultation has a long and healthy tradition in the healing arts, especially in the area of mental health. Two therapists "consult" about the patient of one, a teacher "consults" with a school psychologist about a problem child, and a clergyman "consults" with a psychologist about a problem posed by a parishioner or a problem colleague in his church. What, if anything, do these types of consultations have to do with the kind of organizational consultation with which we are concerned?

In his definitive book on mental health consultation, Caplan (1970) restricts his use of the term *consultation* to the process of collaboration between two professional persons: the consultant, typically the specialist, and the consultee, who requests the consultant's help with some professional problem which he or she is having difficulty solving and which is seen as within the consultant's area of specialized competence. The professional problem may involve the management or treatment of one or more of the clients of the consultee, or the planning or implementation of a program to cater to such clients. Caplan uses the concept of *client* to denote the lay person who is the primary focus of the consultee's professional practice, such as the teacher's student, the psychologist's, psychiatrist's, or social worker's patient, the minister's parishioner, or the lawyer's client.

Caplan's definition of consultation is further restricted to those professional interactions in which the consultant has no direct responsibility for the client and the responsibility for implementing any remedial plan developed through the course of the consultation remains with the consultee. Further, this type of consultation is aimed not only at helping the consultee with the particular problem under scrutiny but also at increasing the general level of the consultee's competence in this area. While this definition of consultation is obviously applicable to any kind of professional work, Caplan restricts his discussion to work in the mental health field, that is, the promotion of mental health, and the prevention, treatment, and rehabilitation of mental disorders.

In consultation, the basic power relationship between the consultant and the consultee is that of peers. Although the consultant does have expert power in the relationship, the consultee is not obligated to accept the consultant's ideas or suggestions. The consultant has no administrative or professional responsibility for the consultee's work (an important difference from supervisory or educational relationships), and he or she should have no need to modify the consultee's approach to the problem posed. The peer quality of the relationship is further fostered by using consultants from outside the consultee's professional institution and, frequently, from outside the consultee's profession. Thus, a psychiatrist from the medical school may consult with the psychologists in the psychology clinic about their therapy cases or a university psychologist may consult with the nurses in the state hospital about the management of a token economy ward.

Types of Mental Health Consultation

Caplan identifies four primary types within his model of mental health consultation. These are: (a) client-centered case consultation; (b) consultee-centered case consultation; (c) program-centered administrative consultation; and (d) consultee-centered administrative consultation. Let us examine each of these in turn.

In *client-centered case consultation*, the focus is on the consultee's professional problems in dealing with a specific case or group of cases, and this is the most typical of all the types of mental health consultation. The major thrust of client-centered consultation is to help the consultee better understand the nature of the client and the problem that the client is presenting. Thus, a teacher may request the help of a school psychologist with a "problem child" in the classroom. Through dialogue, discussion, and even direct observation of the child, the psychologist will help the teacher decide if the child is malnourished, seeks attention, requires neurological evaluation or parental intervention, or if there is some other cause. The focus of this kind of consultation is to help the teacher understand the particular child who gave rise to the current consultation request, but, even more importantly, to increase the capacity of this teacher to deal more effectively with problem children in the future.

In *consultee-centered case consultation*, primary attention is paid to those aspects of the consultee's own professional behavior which are responsible for his or her having the difficulties which have given rise to the consultation. For example, the consultee therapist may experience difficulty in conducting therapy with alcoholics and thus arrange for a well-known practitioner in the community, reputed to be especially successful with alcoholic clients, to serve as a consultant for several consultation sessions. In each of these sessions, the consultee presents one or more of the alcoholic cases with which he has been working and shows how the therapeutic plan has worked out. In the course of these presentations the consultant may grow to recognize that the consultee tends to be overly accepting of the verbal reassurances offered by his alcoholic patients and unable to recognize the denials and manipulations which tend to characterize these patients. The focus of the consultation thus becomes to help the consultee recognize these particular blind spots and deal with them more effectively in the future.

Caplan differentiates four different kinds of consultee-centered case consultations, those based on: (a) lack of knowledge; (b) lack of skill; (c) lack of self-confidence; and (d) lack of professional objectivity. Our example above is of the fourth type and is the most difficult to deal with. The same lack of objectivity which led to the consultation request may lead to the consultee's being unable or unwilling to hear the consultant's evaluation. In this connection, the similarity of this kind of mental health consultation with the consultation case of the young corporate president presented earlier in this chapter is noteworthy. The skills needed for effective consultee-centered consultation are not particularly different from those need-ed for effective counseling or psychotherapy—effective listening, re-lationship building, nonpunitive feedback, and a superb sense of timing.

In *program-centered administrative consultation*, the professional problem is in the area of planning and administration, that is, how to develop a new program or improve an old one. The consultant is expected to come into the organization, study it and the proposed program (or the problem which the program is intended to solve), and prepare a series of recommendations. Since the impact of this kind of consultation is on the system, the recommendations typi-cally are expected to be written and fairly detailed. As was true of the first two types of consultation, there is no assurance that any of the consultant's recommendations, regardless of their merits, will ever be implemented. A variant is when the consultant is asked to present several lectures or seminars centering on the program(s) for which he or she is noted, targeted on the requesting institution(s), with some opportunity for follow-up, in-depth discussion after-wards.

A psychologist may be asked to present a strategy for introduc-ing a behavior modification program into a home for the retarded. A psychiatrist may be asked to review the organization of the state hospital with respect to the effective delivery of services to the pa-tients. A social worker may be asked how to evaluate the out-reach program aimed at the aged of the community. All of these are examples of program-centered administrative consultations, which are aimed at the institution and its technical problems of delivery services.

In *consultee-centered administrative consultation*, the focus is on the psychological characteristics of the organization that prevent it from developing or carrying out the programs that are required for the accomplishment of its mission. Program-centered administrative consultation tends to be more technical, as the organization does not appear to have the resources for diagnosing and solving its own problems. Consultee-centered administrative consultation, on the other hand, tends to be more psychological, as the organization appears to have the necessary problem-solving resources but seems to be unable to use them effectively. Thus, in consultee-centered administrative consultation, the consultant tends to be concerned with psychological group issues, like poor leadership, unresolved authority problems, lack of role clarity, blocks to effective communication, and so on. It is these group psychological problems that are seen as being at the root of the organization's difficulties and it is they that require the consultant's understanding and intervention.

Caplan notes that consultee-centered administrative consultation is the most complicated, interesting, and demanding type of mental health consultation. It is our feelings that the two case excerpts which appear at the beginning of Chapter 1 of this book can be reexamined as evidence for the validity of this conclusion. The reader can speculate how he or she would proceed in either of these cases to engage in a consultee-centered administrative consultation. What kind of information would it be necessary to obtain about either of these organizations, their goals, programs, policies, administrative structure and functioning, and so on? How would you achieve credibility as an objective, external friendly helper? How could you use the information to help these client systems develop a more effective way of going about doing their work? It is hoped that some partial answers to these questions will emerge as we proceed.

The mental-health consultation model developed by Caplan and briefly presented above provides some greater legitimization for the role of the mental health professional as a consultant, if such legitimization is needed, and also provides, in the consultee-centered administrative consultation portion of the model, one base for conceptualizing and understanding the process of organizational consultation. We shall return to this portion of Caplan's model in the next chapter.

The Consulcube

Another even more comprehensive effort to place consultation into a conceptual framework is provided by Blake and Mouton (1976). They argue that all human behavior, individual, group, and organizational, tends to be cyclical in nature. Within some kind of a time frame, and within specified settings, we can see individuals engaging in much the same behavior. The individual gets up at more-or-less the same time, goes to work at the same time, performs his or her tasks in much the same fashion, returns home at the same time and more-or-less by the same route, and so on. On the problematic side, the alcoholic starts off each day with a drink, although promising himself and others faithfully that "this is the last one," drinks his typical quota, and retires to "sleep it off."

Groups behave according to similar cyclical patterns—we see that family arguments have much the same "words and music" to them—and the patterns tend to occur with fairly regular frequency and often in some discernable form. Organizations, too, have their cycles. Indeed, their cycles are often prescribed not only by custom, but also may be mandated by charter, by-laws, or other legislation.

These cyclical behaviors can become so habituated that they can become automatic or beyond the awareness and control of the persons involved in them. While these cyclical, automatic behaviors are of considerable advantage much of the time (for example, who would want to have to deal seriously with such mundane tasks as tying one's shoes or brushing one's teeth) there are exceptions. The pattern of behavior may have become inappropriate as the situation changes and no longer requires the response, or the response may have strong long-term negative consequences, although it may be momentarily rewarding. The family quarrel may no longer be the most useful way of trying to problem-solve around an important issue, but the group, just as individuals and organizations, may be "locked into" the mode of behavior without understanding its cyclical nature or how to break the cycle.

As a means of understanding consulting behavior, Blake and Mouton argue that all consulting interventions attempt the breaking of these cycles. Thus all interventions on the individual, group, organizational, or community level involve the same general principles, have common tactics and strategies, and should focus on a few crucial themes. Blake and Mouton argue that a tennis coach using videotape feedback to improve on a player's backhand, a therapist interpreting a patient's transference, a sensitivity-group facilitator pointing out how the group is smoothing over conflict, the management consultant suggesting a new pattern of memo distribution, an organizational development consultant pointing out to a management team that they could restructure their task assignments are all attempting to help the client break out of a less-than-useful cycle of behavior.

The Consulcube, depicted in Fig. 2.1, represents an effort by Blake and Mouton to organize and systematize our understanding of the consultation process and of all kinds of professional interventions. The Consulcube obviously involves three dimensions: the kinds of interventions along the vertical axis, the focal issues involved in the intervention along the horizontal axis, and the units of change or the targets of the intervention along the third axis.

Within the Consulcube there are 100 cells, each representing the interface between the target of a consultation, the kind of intervention attempted, and the issue which the consultation is intended to resolve. The coding of the cells of the Consulcube in letters and numbers permits us to place any intervention of consultation by means of these three coordinates. Thus a client-centered or Rogerian counselor working with an individual concerned about his or her vocational future would be intervening at Level D 1, while a team-building meeting involving confrontation to help resolve a morale/cohesion problem between the nursing and psychology staffs at a state hospital would be at level J 3. What the Consulcube permits us to do is see directly how all intervention strategies are connected and the underlying principles upon which they are based.

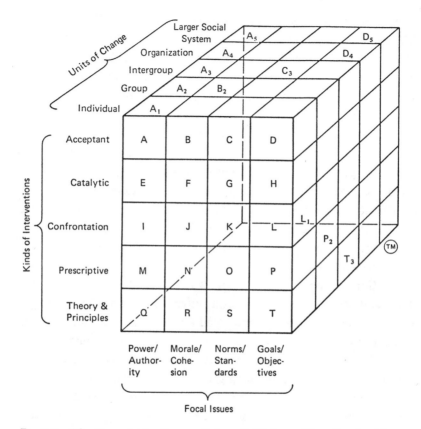

Fig. 2.1   The Consulcube. Source: Robert R. Blake and Jane Srygley Mouton. *Consultation.* Reading, Mass.: Addison-Wesley Publishing Co., 1976, page 7. Reproduced with permission.

It is interesting to note that the Consulcube makes no distinction among the several types of professional workers who are engaged in intervention and consulting activities such as psychologist, psychiatrist, social worker, teacher, pastor, colleague, supervisor, consultant, and so on. Rather they emphasize the underlying strategies on which all these professionals must rely for effective intervention.

Let us begin our analysis on the Consulcube by examining the Units of Change dimension that is concerned with the target of the intervention. Individuals have long sought help with their problems by consulting with a variety of professional persons. Indeed, the beginnings of the mental health movement are found in these needs. Professional workers soon discovered, however, that families, too, were troubled and that individual work could never adequately deal with these family or group problems. Further, workers have developed an entire system of treatment for collections of individuals, sometimes grouped together because of similar problems and sometimes simply out of convenience. Thus, there evolved a system of interventions with groups as their focus rather than individuals.

Groups that exist in the real world—neighbors, work groups, task forces, for example—frequently do not get along very well. Sometimes this is merely an inconvenience as when neighbors find it difficult to coexist comfortably. But in many work situations, collaboration between work groups is imperative for effective accomplishment of the overall task. The management and alleviation of these kinds of intergroup problems also has to be added to the skills of the professional consultant or intervenor.

Organizations are large and complex groups in which there is task and role differentiation. Typically there is a hierarchical structure, there are several sets rather than a single set of norms, and there is a variety of other complexities. While it may not always be clear in any single instance whether we are dealing with an organization or a group, the larger and more complex the system, the more likely it is to be an organization.

Finally, we find larger social systems—such as communities, political units, and multinational corporations—as the final point on our continuum of targets. Blake and Mouton point out that, unfortunately, little has been done on this level, although the need for external intervention in these larger social systems is clearly apparent.

The crux of the Consulcube, however, is the vertical axis which deals with the five major kinds of consulting interventions. As

Blake and Mouton make abundantly clear in their thorough treatment of this point, these five strategies are the major, and perhaps the only, techniques which we have developed for intervening in the affairs of others, regardless of the target of the intervention and regardless of the kind of problems with which we intend to deal.

Acceptant strategies are the first of the interventions considered in the Consulcube. Since many human affairs evoke strong emotional reactions and many of these emotional reactions are negative, the proper management of these feelings is imperative to the accomplishment of one's tasks. Yet we all know that anger, frustration, guilt, and the like simply do not go away, even after considerable time. The emotions can disable us, even when we try to convince ourselves and others that we are not bothered by the feelings any longer.

Acceptant intervention presumes to aid the client(s) through sympathetic listening, empathic understanding, and the clear communication of positive regard for the client who is experiencing psychological discomfort. Such familiar therapeutic procedures as ventilation, catharsis, and reflection of feelings are all specific procedures used by the consultant in his or her acceptant mode of operation.

The following examples illustrate how negative feelings can involve the four different focal issues as we move along the Units of Change dimension from individual to larger social systems: A high school student may be angry at a parent for refusing him the use of the family automobile (power/authority); a work group may be angry at one of its members for consistently showing up late for work (morale/cohesion); labor and management negotiators may disagree about the length of coffee breaks (norms/standards); a charitable organization experiences conflict as it tries to decide its priorities for expending its resources (goals/objectives); and, a national debate may occur on the relative merits of armaments or social welfare as priorities for the future.

Acceptant intervention simply, but importantly, aims at permitting the previously pent-up feelings to surface and be experienced. Underlying the acceptant strategy is the conviction that once these feelings have been fully exposed, the energy that has been expended in covering them up can then be freed for performance of tasks. What the acceptant consultant needs to do in order to accomplish this is be an attentive listener and provide consistent nonevaluative responses. While the consultant may facilitate the release of feelings, it is important that this not be done in any judgmental fashion.

The benefit to the consultee or client is improved self-acceptance, greater spontaneity, the heightened probability of dealing with future emotional problems in more objective terms, a better recognition about the role of emotions in human affairs, and a better, more objective definition of the problem or situation faced, once the overlay of negative emotions has been removed, or at least reduced.

Catalytic interventions are aimed at helping clients gain a better understanding of the situations in which they find themselves by gaining additional information or by verifying existing data. The catalytic consultant aims at increasing the rate at which information is acquired and processed by the client.

Catalytic consultation primarily involves the collection of data about the client by the consultant and the subsequent feeding back of the data to the client. The data can be collected somewhat less formally through interviews and direct observation or more formally through the administration of formal questionnaires and survey instruments. This latter kind of survey feedback is perhaps the most widely practiced kind of organization consultation currently being conducted.

The information collected can deal with any of the four focal issues along the horizontal axis of the Consulcube and may be used to focus on any of the five units of change. Thus, for example, those employees working under a particular supervisor can be interviewed about that supervisor's style of management, especially about how power is used, and the data can be made available to him or her. A morale survey (one involving questions such as "Would you recommend this place to a friend as a good place to work?") could be administered to a work group and then the results of this survey made available for the group itself to discuss. Union and management groups could be asked to describe themselves and each other, using a list of brief phrases or adjectives, and the data could then be shared to help focus on how perceptions had affected the negotiation process. An entire organization might be asked to develop a list of what each member perceives to be the most important things that the organization does and the differences and similarities would be fed back for reaction and discussion in smaller groups. Each of these is an illustration of catalytic intervention at different levels of consultation target.

Catalytic interventions are based upon the assumption that defects in perception are the primary cause of the dysfunction and these misperceptions can be corrected by additional data. The inadequate data base used typically by the client can be improved upon by the consultant, and the task of the consultant is to bring the client and his or her data into a better interface.

The payoff to the client is a modification of perception in the direction of greater clarity. The sharper and less distorted perception, plus the accompanying dialogue, enable the client to solve problems that previously were insoluble.

Confrontational interventions attempt to highlight for the client inappropriate, invalid, or unjustified values by which he or she has been operating and to help the client recognize the underlying values which previously had been ignored, although they did affect the behavior. In a confrontation, the consultant hopes to unravel the underlying values by which the client has been operating and, when appropriate, help the client face the unreality of these values. The client, as most of us, has been previously unable to see that some of his or her deeply held values are inappropriate because of rationalization, denial, justification, projection, and all the other defense mechanisms we use to maintain our self-esteem. The underlying assumption in confrontation is that clients can be helped to understand and recognize their actual values if their behavior is questioned as to why it occurs.

Thus an individual supervisor can be questioned about her supervisory behavior to help her understand that the underlying value of that behavior is that "the boss is always right." A family might be helped to see that it has been smothering real conflict because it believes that family arguments are counterproductive to family harmony. Groups of black and white employees may participate in a racial awareness workshop that forces them to examine the stereotypes that each group has of the other. An organization can be forced to examine if it is really serving the public it has been created to serve, and a nation can question its foreign policy to determine if it represents the country's ideals.

In carrying out a confrontational strategy, the consultant takes nothing for granted as the client describes the situation. Rather, the consultant keeps asking "why does this happen?" until the client begins to examine his or her own underlying values. Further, the consultant challenges the client by presenting facts, counterarguments, and other logical explanations that force the client to recheck his or her thinking. The consultant asks about alternative courses of action, ones that stretch the client's value system and bring it into sharper relief. Finally, the consultant may even offer his or her own solutions, particularly if they are rooted in a different value base, but this should always be done in such a way as to prevent the client from feeling attacked or put down.

The major advantage of the confrontation is that it helps the client examine aspects of behavior that otherwise go unexamined and unrecognized. The role of the consultant in the confrontational mode is always that of the Devil's Advocate, always inquiring why the Emperor chooses to go about naked.

Prescriptive interventions involve the consultant's providing clear directions about what the client should do to solve the problem. A prescriptive consultant operates in a fairly traditional doctor-patient relationship. The success of the consultant in this mode depends on a body of knowledge and skill that permits the consultant to make an accurate diagnosis and develop a plan of corrective action that will solve the client's problem. In contrast with the first three modes of consultation presented, the prescriptive mode requires that the client "buy" both the consultant's diagnosis and the plan of action. Otherwise the consultant has little to offer. Once the consultant is satisfied that the underlying problem has been uncovered, he or she informs the client about what now must be done to solve the problem.

On the individual level, the prescription can be a behavioral change plan for making a supervisor more accessible to his or her subordinates, a training regime to increase a parent's effectiveness, a behavior regime to promote dieting, and so on. On the group level it may be moving a juvenile gang out of the street into the community center or teaching a family how to budget its financial resources. Arbitration, particularly compulsory arbitration, is a prescriptive solution to intergroup conflict. Beyond this, a restructuring of an organization by creating new departments and sections is a solution at the organizational level. Arranging for the dismissal of the top executive of a large social system would be a prescriptive intervention.

Prescriptive consultation is based upon the old adage that "the doctor is always right." There is less opportunity for dialogue and collaboration in this mode than in the others and much depends upon the skill and knowledge of the consultant. An awareness of human fallibility seems to prevent many consultants from heavy reliance upon this mode, especially at the intergroup, organization, and social systems levels of target.

Theory and principles interventions are based on the premise that teaching clients useful theories about their own behavior gives such clients the systematic insight not only to solve their own immediate problems but gives them the resources to solve other problems that may develop in the future. Teaching the client the underlying theory on which the consultant has based his or her practice is one illustration of what George Miller (1969) has termed "the giving away of psychology." By this he means that the knowledge base of our work is shared with those who need it most, freeing them to use our knowledge without our direct help.

Such theory interventions need to be carefully taught. Blake and Mouton strongly argue that the way such theories are taught to the client is critical for the client's understanding and ability to put the theory to future use. The theory needs to be taught experientially and the theory needs to be a truly comprehensive and useful theory, one that provides a cognitive map of the human world in which we live.

Teaching the individual to understand the Managerial Grid (Blake and Mouton, 1964), or teaching McGregor's (1960) views of human motivation (Theory X and Theory Y), or helping an intergroup exercise for understanding alternatives to win-lose strategies, or helping an organization understand Fiedler's (1967) theory of contingent leadership are examples of theory-and-principles-based consultant intervention.

The major problem in teaching clients theories is the inadequacy of our instructional processes, particularly the difficulty we encounter in helping people integrate their learning in such a way that they can actually use the theories in solving their own life problems. Blake and Mouton suggest that, while we have some theories (those noted above) that can help us understand power and authority issues, there is little to guide us in the other three focal issues. Clearly, there is a need for better theoretical understanding in these three areas, whether or not we feel ready to start teaching our theories to our clients for their own use.

What is most impressive about the Consulcube is not its details. Indeed, we shall question Blake and Mouton's choice of the particular four focal issues in Chapter 4. But rather, the Consulcube is a first approximation of an overview of the intervention process, one that places organizational consultation in a matrix of other interventions and helps us understand how such consultations have similar theoretical underpinnings and utilize highly similar intervention strategies.

Dimensions of
Process Consultation

**Process Versus
Content Concerns**

In Chapter 1 we began our
distinction between process and
product concerns. Doubtless you
will recall that by process concerns we mean those interpersonal and group interactions by
which groups and organizations
go about doing their work.
Included among such interactions
would be the attempts, both
successful and unsuccessful, at
communication, influence, and
decision making that are the life
work of organizations. It is important to note that, in this connection, we are not concerned
about the content or *what* of
these communications, influence
attempts, or decisions, but rather
at the *how* of their execution, and
the tensions that remain after
both successful and unsuccessful

efforts. Schein (1969) was the first to label consultation of this sort as *process consultation.*

In process consultation we may be concerned with the patterns of communication, how they have been developed, what they currently are, and how they might be modified so as to reduce the tension, anxiety, and frustration experienced by those who feel that they inappropiately are excluded from such patterns of communication. We might, for instance, discover that certain persons are not routinely included in the distribution of certain classes of memos and that they feel "left out" or rejected by this exclusion. They may not have been included for a variety of reasons—the distribution list may be an old one, one that predates their joining the organization; someone may believe that they do not need the information in that class of memo; or it may be a matter of simple oversight. The important fact is that there is tension resulting from their exclusion and this tension is having negative consequences. In a process consultation, the consultant is never concerned about the content of the memos but rather in whether or not the exclusion of the person is recognized by others. Is the organization willing to "pay the price" for the exclusion? It often turns out that including persons in memo distribution, even though these memos are only of tangential interest to their major responsibility, is a small cost in the maintenance of high group cohesion and harmony. Of course, the change in distribution and the underlying rationale for the change needs to be discussed with those involved. But the point we are making here is that the process consultant is always concerned with how the organization goes about conducting its interpersonal business. This concern is the focus of process consultation.

It seems worthwhile at this juncture to point out that, in the human services area, it is easier for the process consultant to lose his or her focus than it might be in other areas. The psychologist or other mental health professional can observe a staff meeting in a school, a mental health clinic, or a community service agency and actually be able to make a contribution to the topics under discussion, while this is less likely to occur in a staff meeting in an electronics manufacturing plant, an oil refinery, or a restaurant chain. In the human services area, mental health professionals are experts in both the content of the work being carried out and in the process by which it is being done. There is a clear danger that the consultant will begin to function as a content specialist rather than a process specialist, and this lack of role clarity will seriously interfere with his or her effectiveness in attempts to deal with process issues. This problem cannot be overemphasized.

Why does this problem arise? It would seem that an open and thorough examination of process concerns is not usual in any organization, especially in human service delivery agencies which have a pretense of collegiality and closeness. Any serious examination of their process would certainly spoil that pretense. If the consultant begins to operate as a content specialist, then he or she rather quickly may be seen as one of the group, as an outsider with special expertise in the area under discussion, but of no special threat.

When, however, the consultant begins to raise process issues —why was this topic never pursued, how come nobody followed up the lead proposed by so-and-so, how come no one ever responds to this person's questions?—the change in role behavior is unsettling and is much more easily challenged. Who asked this stranger to disrupt our work and ask difficult and impertinent questions? If the process consultant can restrain the impulse to demonstrate his or her content expertise at such times and hold back from intervening until an appropriate process concern can be raised, his or her task will be that much easier. Yet we need to remember that one of the reasons that the particular consultant was able to gain entry into the system might have been that he or she was seen by significant members as having content expertise and thus as being more acceptable as a consultant. These issues need to be thoroughly explored by client and consultant early in the consulting process. It is strongly recommended that process consultants use their content expertise as a background by which they better observe and understand how the client organization proceeds to do its work rather than help them do that work directly.

While we will return to the issues involved in the consultant's entry into the client system in Chapter 5, we need to point out here that this concept of process consultation is a difficult one to communicate to naive client systems (and most of them are naive) and this lack of conceptual clarity on the client's part makes the entry of the consultant on a process basis rather difficult. While one might like to believe that human service delivery systems ought to be rather knowledgeable and sympathetic to a process approach to understanding their internal workings and thus welcome the process-oriented consultant, this rarely turns out to be the case. Our experience has been that these human service systems are the most resistant to process consultation, protesting that they have no troublesome interpersonal or group interactions, that their own internal resources would be adequate to handle them if they did, and in any event, they doubt the competence of these external process consultants. They quibble about the theoretical model the consultant might be proposing, inquire about the reliability of the consultant's instruments, and demand "proof" about the potential outcome of the intervention. This strongly suggests that human service delivery systems are no more immune from process concerns than are other kinds of organizations.

On the other hand, organizations in the business-industrial sector, while clearly apprehensive about the arcane skills and procedures of the process consultant and quite anxious about being "psyched out," are much more willing to own up to the fact that there are internal interpersonal and intergroup issues that are interfering with the total effectiveness of the organization, and they are typically more open to process consultation despite their prior lack of exposure. For organizations in the private sector, process consultation is seen as a potential tool for resolving problems interfering

with productivity and profit, and a turn-around in these criteria
will provide evidence of effective consultation.

Organizations in the public and third sectors often ask for consultant help as content specialists as noted in the introductory chapter.
If more generic issues tend to emerge over time, the consultant
attempts to change his or her role from a content to a process
orientation, a serious and difficult undertaking. It is of critical
importance that both the client and the consultant, especially the
latter, be aware of what role the consultant is playing at any moment of time. Another approach to consultation requests, however,
is that of the consumer who knows what is needed and is attempting to find a purveyor of that commodity. This approach to
consultation occurs in all kinds of organizations as they attempt to
keep up with the latest in management technology. They ask for
consultants to carry out communication-skills workshops, to train
their management personnel in management-by-objectives or cost-
benefit analysis, in transactional analysis, or whatever the latest
management journals have covered.

In this consumer approach to the use of consultants, the success
of the consultation will depend upon: (a) the adequacy of the
client's self-diagnosis; (b) the degree to which the client has adequately communicated the diagnosis to the consultant; (c) the adequacy of the consultant's skills for providing the services required;
and, (d) the impact of the requested services on the client system
after receipt of the services. But, the raising of such questions is, in
itself, a process approach and there are all too many consultant
organizations with packaged programs which they market and sell
to whomever they can. The underlying assumption of the consumer
approach to consultation is the traditional one of the marketplace,
"The customer is always right."

Still another approach to consultation is the medical one, one
that assumes a doctor–patient relationship between consultant and
client. In the medical model, the client surrenders responsibility for

the organization or system to the consultant. The consultant is brought in to examine the client system, make recommendations, and then carry them out. The client identifies what is believed to be the issue but these are typically presented in symptomatic terms. Thus the consultant may be told, "We have high turnover in the administrative services department," or "We get a lot of complaints about the workers in the registration area." Or, the presentation might be even more simple, "Look us over and tell us what you think."

In this medical model, the success of the consultation will depend upon: (a) the diagnostic skill of the consultant, recognizing that there will be little trust and the diagnostic information made available to the consultant will almost always be distorted; (b) the ability of the consultant to adequately communicate the diagnosis arrived at; (c) the ability of the consultant to develop an adequate intervention plan based upon that diagnosis; and, (d) the ability of the consultant to carry out the intervention plan on a passive, if not resistant, client system.

While the medical model of consultation may appear at first glance to be similar to the process consultation approach, this similarity is quite superficial. Indeed, one, if not the primary, characteristic of process consultation is the collaborative nature of the relationship between the client and the consultant. The consultant's role in this collaboration is principally a facilitative and coordinating one. Most process consultants strongly warn against assuming responsibility for the client system, responsibility which must be the client's in the long run and thus cannot be assumed by the consultant, even for a short period of time. Consultants must take responsibility for their own behavior and its consequences, but not for the client or the client's problems.

In contrast to both the consumer and medical models of consultation, this collaboration between client and consultant is important throughout the consultation relationship. The diagnosis of the client system is a joint one, understood and agreed to by both parties.

The intervention is jointly implemented by the client and consultant, even though the consultant may have been more involved in developing the idea of the plan due to his or her greater familiarity with such technology. The process of evaluating the outcomes of the intervention and the termination of the relationship between client and consultant are likewise shared responsibilities in process consultation and, at every stage, the consultant has an obligation to initiate a process evaluation of what has transpired thus far in the consulting relationship and the degree of satisfaction of both partners. If there is less than a high level of satisfaction, their relationship needs to be the next issue for the client and consultant to address, or the consultant needs to consider the wisdom of continuing the relationship.

Thus, the basic assumption of process consultation is that the client must be helped to identify his or her own issues, to share in the diagnosis, and to be actively involved in the development of a solution. It is hoped that in this fashion the consultant aids the client not only in solving the immediate problem but also in developing better problem-identification and problem-solving skills for the future. While the consultant may play a major role in focusing the diagnosis and in suggesting alternative solutions because of his or her greater expertise in such matters, the client always has the final and complete responsibility for accepting or declining these inputs.

The expertise of the process consultant is thus not in the particular problems that the client system is encountering but rather in the facilitative skills of helping self-exploration and self-discovery. The process consultant must know how to set a climate enabling the client to engage in a focused and in-depth self-analysis, one in which the discovery of issues and concerns that have long been avoided is possible. The opening up of such issues is not the cause for either self-blame or a search for scapegoats, but rather the occasion for relief and the release of energy for problem solving of long-delayed concerns. Process consultants in their collaborative relations with clients may often determine that there is a need for a content expert, for someone with expertise in curriculum development, new methods of behavior modification, or some new management process, but it is the role of the process consultant to assist in articulating the need rather than to fill it. The primary expertise of the process consultant is the development and maintainence of a helping relationship.

Value Issues in Organizational Consultation

Thus far we have been discussing process consultation, if not all of organizational consultation, in terms of its procedures and technology as though there were no underlying values involved. This, of course, is not the case. Organizational consultants, like psychotherapists and other professionals, always operate from a strong, personal value orientation. Further, those of us involved in process consultation tend to operate from a fairly explicit and reasonably well-articulated set of values.

The values that have emerged from process consultation, or perhaps the values that have led to the development of it, include a belief in the value of a collaborative approach in the conduct and management of human affairs. This kind of collaborative approach requires a commitment to democratic social structures and can be effective only where there are humanized interpersonal relationships. This requires a high degree of authenticity.

Equally important in process consultation is the belief that there needs to be a reasonable degree of congruence between the demands of the organization and the personal needs of the members of that organization, that the discrepancy between these organizational demands and personal needs must be openly examined, and that whatever discrepancies are uncovered then require joint attention by the organization and its members in order to reduce them.

Since most organizations have considerable discrepancies between their demands and the needs of their members, process consultation has broadened into an approach to planned social change which has come to be known as Organization Development (OD). OD covers all those attempts to change an organization's culture from one in which there is avoidance of any examination of social processes, such as communication, planning, and decision making, to one that institutionalizes and legitimizes this kind of self-examination. Further, OD involves the changing of an organization from one that resists change to one that promotes the planning and use of procedures for adapting to needed changes on a regular basis.

While there is no single, agreed-upon definition of OD, the general thrust of the many definitions can be seen in those by Burke and Schmidt (1971), "Organizational development is conceived as a process for increasing organizational effectiveness by integrating individual needs and desires for growth with organizational goals, using the knowledges and techniques of the behavioral sciences," and by Schmuck (1976), "OD can be defined as a planned and sustained effort in process consultation to apply behavioral science concepts and techniques for system improvement using reflexive, self-analytic methods." These two definitions clearly indicate the planned-change goals of OD, the reliance on process consultation, and the behavioral-science base from which OD attempts to operate.

OD can thus be seen as the more generic, the more inclusive term, one which involves a variety of change activities and may include such changes as job enrichment, modification of the work environment, changing administrative reporting lines, and so on. But what needs to be recognized is that process consultation is typically regarded as the critical ingredient in an OD process as it initiates a collaborative norm—one that involves consultant and clients, supervisors and direct labor, different work groups—that is necessary for the diagnosis, planning, and execution of the OD change strategy. Without process consultation as a catalyst for the "opening up" of channels of dialogue, any organizational change is simply change, one which may or may not be accepted, one which may or may not have the desired effects. But with a process consultation initiation of the planned change, there is broad collaborative involvement and the commitment that this collaboration generates produces a clearly predictable outcome.

Organization development needs to be clearly differentiated from Management Development or MD. In MD the focus is on training the individual manager and developing his or her individual management skills without much attention to the particular organizational context in which these skills will be applied (Goodstein, 1971). OD, on the other hand, focuses on the training of intact organizational units. So we see that the focus of MD is an individual one while the focus of OD is an organizational one. While MD assumes that the participants in management training programs, typically carried on away from the work site, will have enhanced skills and greater competence at the conclusion of such training, the utilization of those skills in the work place are ordinarily not given much attention. Also, those organizational issues which may either interfere with the managerial competence of that individual manager or might facilitate his or her development as a manager are overlooked.

Thus OD aims at developing functional organizational procedures in a supportive environment within the organization in which group problem solving can occur. Team building, or training the organizational unit(s) in more effective interpersonal relations, and clarifying the role relationship of members of the unit, especially among the members of intact, working units, lies at the heart of this kind of OD. And, obviously, this kind of training needs to be preceded by process consultation. We will return to further discussion of the techniques of team building in Chapter 7, but it can readily be seen that such team building of organizational units can occur only as part of an OD intervention and that the intrinsic values of such an intervention are collaboration, openness, and sharing of power and authority.

Another way in which the values of process consultation, and OD, can be seen is through an examination of Douglas McGregor's (1960) descriptions of two archetypical management philosophies —Theory X and Theory Y. Theory X, the more traditional view, is based on the assumptions that people are, by nature, lazy and will work as little as possible; that people are lacking in ambition, shun responsibility, and prefer to be led; that people are self-centered and indifferent to organizations and their needs; that people are resistant to change; and that people are gullible, unintelligent, and easily duped or cheated. This set of assumptions leads management, as the responsible party involved, to direct people, motivate them, control their behavior, and change their behavior to fit the needs of the organization, for, without this active stance by management, people would be passive or even resistant to organizational needs. Thus the proper role of management is to persuade, reward, punish, and control people, all in the direction of controlling their behavior to meet organizational goals.

Theory Y, on the other hand, assumes that the expenditure of energy, both mental and physical, is as natural for humans as play or rest; that people will exercise control to achieve goals to which they are committed; that this commitment to goals requires that personal satisfaction, especially self-respect, be associated with the attainment of these goals; that people seek, not avoid, responsibility; that most people have a degree of imagination, ingenuity, creativity, and intelligence to bring to bear on organizational problems; and that these potentials are only partially utilized in most modern organizations. This rather different set of assumptions leads management to see its task as the arrangement of organizational conditions and procedures of operation so that people can achieve their own goals best by the attainment of organizational objectives. By this, of course, McGregor meant a democratic, participative, joint decision making, and self-controlling rather than supervisor-controlling kind of leadership.

While arguments about the basic nature of people are probably as old as humankind itself, what is different about McGregor's argument is his assertion that the extant research evidence reported in the psychological literature strongly supports Theory Y. Thus, McGregor argues that Theory Y is not simply a value commitment, but an empirically supported value commitment. And, indeed, Miner (1963), in summarizing the pertinent evidence, has concluded that those supervisors who delegate tasks to subordinates are more likely to have these tasks accomplished and those supervisors who show strong concern for their subordinates as human beings will have higher performance records. Further, almost all of the studies (e.g., Bowers, 1965; Likert, 1961; Trist et al., 1963) tend to support strongly the theoretical base for Theory Y management behavior.

It is important to recognize that Theory Y is not a soft approach to management. Rather it is a demanding style in which it is assumed that workers wish to and can produce. It sets high standards for all and expects the standards to be achieved. Clearly most organizations are not managed from a Theory Y stance and the transition from the more typical Theory X to a Theory Y process is difficult for both workers and management as they attempt to change both their behavior and their attitudes. But Theory Y managers, as part of their orientation, must see people as growing and developing, with a good capacity for making beneficial kinds of changes.

Process consultation, and indeed, the entire OD enterprise, is strongly wedded to the development and support of Theory Y. While there are portions of McGregor's argument that one can take exception to, it represents one of the earliest and strongest value statements, one that has had enormous impact upon the field of organizational consultation. This is true not only for the explicit values that McGregor has articulated but also is a case for turning to the research literature as the base of support for accepting or rejecting a position. McGregor must be seen as one of the leaders both in the development of an articulated value system and also in the field of applied behavioral science.

Another insight into the values of organizational development can be gained by an examination of how organizational consultants view their client organizations. Fordyce and Weil (1971), two experienced organizational consultants, have developed a set of characteristics of "healthy" and "unhealthy" organizations that is presented in Table 3.1.

Table 3.1   Some Characteristics of Unhealthy and Healthy Organizations

Unhealthy	*Healthy*
1. Little personal investment in organizational objectives except at top levels.	1. Objectives are widely shared by the members and there is a strong and consistent flow of energy toward those objectives.
2. People in the organization see things going wrong and do nothing about it. Nobody volunteers. Mistakes and problems are habitually hidden or shelved. People talk about office troubles at home or in the halls, not with those involved.	2. People feel free to signal their awareness of difficulties because they expect the problems to be dealt with and they are optimistic that they can be solved.
3. Extraneous factors complicate problem-solving. Status and boxes on the organization chart are more important than solving the problem. There is an excessive concern with management as a customer, instead of the real customer. People treat each other in a formal and polite manner that masks issues— especially with the boss. Nonconformity is frowned upon.	3. Problem-solving is highly pragmatic. In attacking problems, people work informally and are not preoccupied with status, territory, or second-guessing "what higher management will think." The boss is frequently challenged. A great deal of nonconforming behavior is tolerated.
4. People at the top try to control as many decisions as possible. They become bottlenecks, and make decisions with inadequate information and advice. People	4. The points of decision-making are determined by such factors as ability, sense of responsibility, availability of information, work load, timing, and require-

Unhealthy	*Healthy*
complain about managers' irrational decisions.	ments for professional and management development. Organizational level as such is not considered a factor.
5. Managers feel alone in trying to get things done. Somehow orders, policies, and procedures don't get carried out as intended.	5. There is a noticeable sense of team play in planning, in performance, and in discipline—in short, a sharing of responsibility.
6. The judgment of people lower down in the organization is not respected outside the narrow limits of their jobs.	6. The judgment of people lower down in the organization is respected.
7. Personal needs and feelings are side issues.	7. The range of problems tackled includes personal needs and human relationships.
8. People compete when they need to collaborate. They are very jealous of their area of responsibility. Seeking or accepting help is felt to be a sign of weakness. Offering help is unthought of. They distrust each other's motives and speak poorly of one another; the manager tolerates this.	8. Collaboration is freely entered into. People readily request the help of others and are willing to give in turn. Ways of helping one another are highly developed. Individuals and groups compete with one another, but they do so fairly and in the direction of a shared goal.
9. When there is a crisis, people withdraw or start blaming one another.	9. When there is a crisis, the people quickly band together in work until the crisis departs.
10. Conflict is mostly covert and managed by office politics and other games, or there are interminable and irreconcilable arguments.	10. Conflicts are considered important to decision-making and personal growth. They are dealt with effectively, in the open. People say what they want and expect others to do the same.
11. Learning is difficult. People don't approach their peers to learn from them, but have to learn by their own mistakes; they reject the experience of others. They get little feedback on performance, and much of that is not helpful.	11. There is a great deal of on-the-job learning based on a willingness to give, seek, and use feedback and advice. People see themselves and others as capable of significant personal development and growth.

Unhealthy	Healthy
12. Feedback is avoided.	12. Joint critique of progress is routine.
13. Relationships are contaminated by maskmanship and image building. People feel alone and lack of concern for one another. There is an undercurrent of fear.	13. Relationships are honest. People do care about one another and do not feel alone.
14. People feel locked into their jobs. They feel stale and bored but constrained by the need for security. Their behavior, for example in staff meetings, is listless and docile. It's not much fun. They get their kicks elsewhere.	14. People are "turned on" and highly involved by choice. They are optimistic. The work place is important and fun (why not?).
15. The manager is a prescribing father to the organization.	15. Leadership is flexible, shifting in style and person to suit the situation.
16. The manager tightly controls small expenditures and demands excessive justification. He allows little freedom for making mistakes.	16. There is a high degree of trust among people and a sense of freedom and mutual responsibility. People generally know what is important to the organization and what isn't.
17. Minimizing risk has a very high value.	17. Risk is accepted as a condition of growth and change.
18. "One mistake and you're out."	18. "What can we learn from each mistake?"
19. Poor performance is glossed over or handled arbitrarily.	19. Poor performance is confronted, and a joint resolution sought.
20. Organization structure, policies, and procedures encumber the organization. People take refuge in policies and procedures, and play games with organization structure.	20. Organization structure, procedures, and policies are fashioned to help people get the job done and to protect the long-term health of the organization, not to give each bureaucrat his due. They are also readily changed.
21. Tradition!	21. There is a sense of order, and yet a high rate of innovation. Old methods are questioned and often give way.

Unhealthy	Healthy
22. Innovation is not widespread, but in the hands of only a few.	22. The organization itself adapts swiftly to opportunities or other changes in its market-place because every pair of eyes is watching and every head is anticipating the future.
23. People swallow their frustrations: "I can do nothing. It's their responsibility to save the ship."	23. Frustrations are the call to action. "It's my/our responsibility to save the ship."

Source: J.K. Fordyce, and R. Weil, *Managing with people*. Reading, Mass.: Addison-Wesley, 1971, pp. 11–14. Reproduced with permission.

A close inspection of these 23 pairs of characteristics clearly reveals the implicit set of values upon which Fordyce and Weil, and most other organizational consultants, tend to operate. The importance of openness, democracy, flexibility of role, high congruence between personal and organizational goals, and high personal commitment to organizational values would all seem to emerge as underlying values. Traditional, role-specified, hierarchical organizations that do not prize openness or that see conflict as facilitating the development of stronger personal commitment to organizational goals (this includes most organizations in the business of delivering human services) do not fare well when evaluated against these criteria.

If most consultants have rather different values from their clients, then we can readily understand many of the problems that both organizational consultants and their clients encounter at every stage of the consultation process. These value discrepancies will be obvious when the consultant attempts to enter the client organization and is engaged in the diagnostic process and in the development of strategies to bring about change. We shall examine these discrepancies and how they need to be managed in the last four chapters of this book.

Process Consultation and Other Models of Consultation

In Chapter 2 we examined Caplan's (1970) Mental Health Consultation and Blake and Mouton's (1976) Consulcube. How is process consultation different from and similar to these two models?

While Caplan does not use the term *process consultation* himself, it should be reasonably clear that his consultee-centered administrative consultation is highly similar to process consultation. It can be recalled that Caplan sees this mode of mental health consultation as helping the client system implement organizational programs which had been blocked because of internal problems. "The consultant centers his attention primarily on the work difficulties of the consultees and attempts to help them improve their problem-solving skills and overcome their shortcomings" (Caplan, 1970, p. 165). Thus, the intent and target of consultee-centered administrative consultation is very similar to that of process consultation.

While it is difficult to determine the degree of similarity in the actual execution of this mode of administrative consultation and process consultation, Caplan makes one critical point that does suggest considerable similarity when he states, ". . . I restrict my intervention to increasing the range and depth of their understanding of the issues and to augmenting their emotional capacity to use such knowledge productively. It is then up to them to work out solutions in the light of their own personal and role-related choices (p. 275)." While one might argue that the process consultation would be more clearly committed to a collaborative development of a solution, Caplan is addressing himself to *process* issues in his dealing with his clients. This similarity is further heightened when one reviews the six major intervention strategies which Caplan lists: (1) increase mastery by extending consultee's cognitive field; (2) increase mastery of feelings; (3) improve communications; (4) reduce perceptual distortions; (5) improve leadership; and (6) increase congruence of satisfaction of personal and organizational needs. Although there may be differences between Caplan's personal style of consultation and that of others who consider themselves process consultants, it would seem safe to include Caplan as one of them, at least when he functions in his consultee-centered administrative model.

Blake and Mouton (1976) in their presentation of the Consulcube do specifically deal with process consultation. They see it as a catalytic intervention, one that can focus on any of the five targets—individual, group, intergroup, organizational, or larger social system—and one that can involve any of the four focal issues—power/authority, morale/cohesion, norms/standards, or goals/objectives. In this connection we need to remember that Blake and Mouton see catalytic interventions as speeding up the procedure by which data is processed by the client system. Thus, the role of the catalytic or process consultant, according to Blake and Mouton, is to bring data into clearer focus, especially data which had previously been systematically overlooked or uncommunicated. One important assumption operating here is that more information about the problem under scrutiny will modify the client's perception of the situation. Therefore, according to Blake and Mouton, the process or catalytic consultant tends to focus on the gathering and feeding back of information in ways that the client usually does not use.

An example may make this point clearer. Virtually all work tends to get processed, that is, analyzed and discussed by those who perform it. Who has not shared with a colleague one's concern, frustration, and anger after attending a poorly run meeting? But our typical norm is that this kind of *processing* or analyzing of the work of the meeting is never openly discussed as part of the agenda of the meeting itself. Instead, the processing is done informally, over coffee after the meeting, at the bar during a TGIF rendezvous, or in some other informal, nonwork setting. Naturally one of the negative consequences of this kind of processing is that it never affects the work discussed in the future. The process consultant's job is to arrange for processing ("How do we feel this meeting has been going?") to be included as part of the official agenda of the meeting.

The processing can be initiated by having the consultant raise the question for open discussion or have post-meeting questionnaires filled out and discussed at the next meeting. The important point is that the information is made available to the client system and can then catalyze or speed up the information processing. It is for these reasons that Blake and Mouton regard the process consultant as primarily catalytic in nature.

While it is difficult to argue with this position, it should be noted that process consultation may involve a variety of intervention strategies that may be used simultaneously. The process consultant clearly needs to be acceptant, especially early in the consultation process, but also throughout the intervention, although perhaps more important, the role is a catalytic one. In our example, we see the attempts to change norms and standards. The consultant is trying to change the organization's norms from a closed and informal processing of meetings to an open and formal one. Perhaps variations on the Consulcube model can best be seen as the inherent difficulties involved in any system that attempts to place complex and involved human behaviors into pigeon holes, even three-dimensional ones.

In closing this discussion, it would seem apparent that, while Caplan and Blake and Mouton have included process consultation in their overall schema of consultation, they have not accorded process consultation the central and primary role that we accord it.

Some Approaches to Understanding Organizations

Need for Understanding Organizations

The process model of consultation we have described always involves a collaboration between the consultant and the client system. Certainly, one of the attributes that the consultant should bring to that collaboration is an in-depth understanding of organizations and how they function. As we know, the consultant needs to avoid being seen as a content specialist but at the same time must give the client confidence that he or she does understand organizations and how they work. What the consultant needs, therefore, is a good theory of organizations. As we know, the consultant one of the fathers of the social psychology of organizational life, once remarked, "There is nothing so practical as a good theory." Such a theory would suggest potential sources of data to help understand the problem, ways of organizing and conceptualizing the data, and, finally, routes toward an effective solution to the problem. It would be very helpful in this context if we could provide a theory of organizations. Indeed, it would be even better if we could present *the* theory of organizations. But, alas, this is not to be. There are perhaps as many theories of organizational behavior as there are theorists and, while each tends to proclaim the general utility of its approach, the personal predilections of the consultant appear to be the most common basis for accepting one over any other.

Many readers will see the similarity between the theories of organizational behavior and those of personality, or individual behavior. Clearly a good theory of personality is essential for the development and practice of counseling and psychotherapy. Yet there are many theories of personality and they lead therapists into exploring different aspects of their client's behavior, using different therapeutic approaches, and even applying different criteria to judge their success. The lack of a unified theory of organizational behavior has led to the same state of affairs in organizational consultation. Consultants tend to examine different aspects of organizational life, use different outcomes as instances of their success—all based upon their own theoretical view of organizational behavior. This is true even among those consultants who operate from a process consultation model, for the commitment to this model is possible in combination with a variety of theoretical points of view about other aspects of organizational life.

One of the major differences between organizational and personality theory, however, is that fewer organizational theories are generally available, especially to the public. There are few educated adults who do not have an operating theory of personality, a way of examining and understanding human behavior. While this theory may or may not be explicit and labeled, we see such theories in operation when we participate in discussions of why Bob and Mary got divorced, why Bill is unhappy in his job, why Fred and Martha seem to have so much trouble in handling their children, why Ann ought to get promoted, and so on. On the other hand, we seem to have few such discussions about organizational behavior and most of us appear not to have any implicit theory of organizational life.

We seem to be an individually oriented society and much of our approach to understanding behavior is in terms of the individuals involved and their intra- and interpersonal dynamics. Our mass media—newspapers and radio, TV news and TV soap operas— typically focus our attention on the individual and on his or her motivation. Very seldom is the focus on group or organizational issues. We have been exposed to a long and intensive training in developing an understanding of individual behavior, but we do not learn to understand organizations and how they work.

In order to help remedy this gap in our knowledge we will present fairly brief overviews of a number of different approaches to understanding organizational life. It is questionable whether any of them can be regarded as theories. Mostly, they tend to be ways of approaching and understanding organizations and they vary markedly in completeness. The reader should note that we are not suggesting that this brief overview represents the complete range of ideas on organizations. Rather, there are represented different points of view that seem to have some direct relevance for the consulting process. There will be a good bit of overlap among these ideas. It is hoped the overlap and redundancy will be seen as indices of the importance placed on certain aspects of organizational life; the unique portions of each point of view indicates the specific contributions of that approach.

An Open-Systems Approach to Understanding Organizations

Perhaps the most complete, as well as the most complex, approach to understanding human organizations is one based on open-systems theory and presented by Daniel Katz and Robert L. Kahn in *The Social Psychology of Organizations* (1966). Open-systems theory, originally proposed by von Bertalanffy (1956), sees social systems as patterns of recurrent activities in which energy (information, raw materials, personnel, and so on) is imported into the system and transformed in some fashion or other, and the resulting product is exported back into the environment. Open-systems theory is concerned with the relationships between elements of the system, with the structure of the system, and with the interdependence of the system, especially as each of these effect the energy transformation process. Further, open-systems theory was proposed as an alternative to closed-systems notions, that is, systems which operate according to the laws of classical Newtonian physics. In contrast to closed systems, open systems maintain themselves through constant commerce with their environment, that is, a continual exchange of energy between the two.

The functioning of any open system thus consists of recurrent cycles of input, transformation, and output. While the transformation process is wholly contained within the open system, both the input and output involves dealing with the external environment. A smoothly functioning open system requires a good balance between the input and output requirements so that the system can receive adequate and continual input from the environment and its output can be absorbed by the same environment. As one simple example of this approach, consider the typical university with its cycle of admitting new students at the beginning of each academic year, transforming them into educated persons, and then graduating them into an accepting society. We can note the cyclic nature of this process, the need for a match between input and output characteristics, and how there is a continual exchange of energy with the environment—funds, new faculty, books and journals, and so on.

According to open-systems theory, the most important aspect of the system is the transformation process, but this process can function competently only when the system restricts its input to energy or materials that it can transform and, similarly, restricts its output to that which the environment can accept. Levinson and Astrachan (1976) point how the intake service of a community mental health center is responsible for monitoring the organization's boundaries so that an adequate client population is received from the community and for making certain that there is an adequate link between the newly admitted client and the treatment providers.

Open systems are further characterized by: (a) negative entropy, that is, strong countervailing forces against the natural tendency of all systems to run down; (b) feedback or responsiveness to information about its own effectiveness; (c) homeostasis, or continual efforts to maintain a steady state; (d) equifinality, or the use of different patterns to produce the same effect; and (e) differentiation, or the tendency to elaborate the structure of the system.

But human organizations lack structure in any anatomical sense. Instead there are patterns of behavioral events that give them stability and order. Thus, when we apply open-systems theory to organizations, we are struck by the importance of the *role* behavior of the organization's members, the organizational *norms* prescribing and sanctioning these behaviors, and the *values* in which these norms are embedded. Roles are sets of functionally specific, interrelated behaviors generated by interrelated tasks. Role behaviors are carried out, not because of the personal needs of the individual, but because they are necessary for the system. In all organizations these roles quickly become habitually accepted and serve to set the task demands for those who occupy the roles. Thus organizations can be seen as a series of interrelated or overlapping roles, each of which is dependent upon the other for the organization to maintain its viability. At least on this level, organizations are structures of roles.

If we accept the implied importance of roles in organizations, then we can understand why these roles are surrounded by strong belief systems about their appropriateness and why organizations develop powerful sanctions to maintain what is regarded as appropriate role behavior. "That's the way we do it here," "If you don't like it, get out!" Statements such as these are only the more obvious examples of the way roles are monitored by organizations. Thus norms and values are those commonly held beliefs of an evaluative sort that support and maintain role behavior. Values are the more general or elaborate forms of these beliefs and norms the more specific.

What are the implications of such an open-systems approach to organizational life for consultants? The most direct and clear-cut implication is that the roles involved in any particular organization, the fashion in which these roles are imparted, the clarity of role behaviors, the smoothness of the interrelationship among the several roles, and the underlying norms and values which support these roles are the most important foci of the consultant's attention, both in the diagnostic and intervention phases of the consultation.

In their presentation of the applications of open-systems theory to organizations, however, Katz and Kahn do not limit themselves to a concern with just roles, norms, and values. They also identify several other critical areas of organizations that need to be understood, although in each case their analysis is couched in terms of open-systems theory. One such area is the power and authority structure of the organization, by which they mean the supervision and review of organizationally required action, and the exertion of corrective or innovative influence as necessary. Thus, someone must act when additional resources—money or personnel—are needed or when the organizational structure turns out to be nonfunctional. Another area is communication or the flow of information in the organization, especially that which is necessary for effectiveness. Still another area is the formulation of organizational policy and the making of decisions. By policymaking they mean the creation of general statements about what organizational behavior shall be, that is, the formulation of goals and objectives and the formulation of strategies and procedures for achieving and assessing progress toward such goals. Lastly, Katz and Kahn identify leadership or acts of influence on matters of organizational relevance as a final area of concern. These four areas—power and authority, communications, policy formulation and decision making, and leadership—are additional concerns for the organizational consultant to focus his or her attention on in addition to roles, norms, and values.

The Tavistock Institute and Psychoanalytic Approaches

The general impact of psychoanalysis on the behavioral sciences has been so broad that it is difficult to specify its effect on our understanding of organizations. One highly relevant point is the importance placed on unconscious processes in both individual and group behavior (Rice, 1965). The work of Bion (1961) clearly suggests that such psychoanalytic phenomena as resistance, transference, and projection were found in groups as well as individuals, and probably in organizations as well.

The Tavistock Institute of London has been a center for the development of a psychoanalytic theory of organizations (Rice, 1963, 1969). Much of the work of the Tavistock staff has been on the study group or small work conference in which the participants are helped to learn about how they and others deal with issues of authority and leadership under clear-cut boundary conditions. When the expectations of the participants for emotional gratification (direction, support, encouragement, and such) from the study-group staff (or consultants) are not met, a variety of issues surface—concern about competency, both staff and participant, concern over participant responsibility, fears of the irrational, anger, and so on. The discussion of these phenomena by the participants and consultants during the latter stages of the study conferences is aimed at helping those present understand back-home organizational issues.

The Tavistock study group, with its focus on the management of boundary conditions, role relationships, especially those involving power and authority, and the importance of unconscious processes, highlights the Tavistock approach to understanding organizational behavior. Perhaps the most central consideration is that of boundary condition management. Effective organizations are seen as those with boundaries that are permeable to those exchanges necessary for task accomplishment and impermeable to those exchanges which inhibit task performance.

Organizations establish boundaries between themselves and the environment in which they exist. These can be physical boundaries—high walls, guarded gates, visits by invitation only—or psychological boundaries—forbidding environment, unfriendly receptionists, long waits for appointments. Organizational sites located far from population centers, requiring uniforms that distinguish members from the rest of the population, and having to speak to several secretaries prior to speaking to a key person in an organization are also examples of psychological boundaries. The community mental health movement may be seen as an effort to make the boundaries of mental health delivery systems more permeable. As Levinson and Astrachan (1976) note, however, the way the admissions are handled is crucial in determining whether or not the boundary conditions are indeed more permeable. In all such situations, however, the question is whether or not the established boundary conditions facilitate or inhibit work attainment. Thus, too many patients can "flood" the treatment system while too few cause it to dry up.

Organizations also establish internal boundaries. Departments, divisions, sections, and other groups are established, usually on a relatively permanent basis, and these are typically based on some division of labor. Thus, purchasing and manufacturing, psychology and English, pediatrics and gynecology are typically separated, with both physical and psychological boundaries between them. As was the case with external boundaries, the major concern is with the functional nature of these internal boundaries—do they help or hinder getting the job done? It is interesting to note that those jobs in organizations which involve managing the boundary conditions—either internal or external—typically involve much more conflict than those "deeper" in the organization (Kahn et al., 1964), suggesting that such boundary management does involve personal stress.

One aspect of organizational life of special interest to the Tavistock group is the relationship between the structural way in which the work force is organized and social-psychological relationships among the workers. Rice (1958) and his colleagues at Tavistock base their organizational consultations on three major assumptions: (1) tasks should be organized so that those involved are able to complete the task themselves; (2) tasks should be organized so that the work activities may be controlled by the workers themselves; (3) related tasks should be organized so that the workers involved in these tasks can have mutually satisfying relationships. Two additional, but less critical, assumptions are also involved: (1) the most effective work group is one containing the fewest people necessary to complete the entire task; and (2) the most stable work group is one with the fewest differences in status, one in which the skills necessary to perform the task are understood and aspired to by all members of the group. These concerns can be seen as specific ways of managing internal boundary conditions within an organization and are thus theoretically derived from the general position of the Tavistock group. It can also be noted that there is strong research support (e.g., Rice, 1958) for the contention that these are the characteristics of effective organizations.

The Consulcube

While the approaches to understanding organizations derived from open-systems theory and psychoanalysis can be regarded as more-

or-less theoretical, the remainder of the approaches to be covered in this chapter are more empirically derived. In other words, the experience of the consultants has, in some way, convinced them of the importance of these variables and they recommend that other consultants consider them in their work.

The reader will recall that in the Consulcube four focal issues were identified: power/authority, morale/cohesion, norms/standards, and goals/objectives. Blake and Mouton (1976) note that these four focal issues are interdependent so that a change in one of them is likely to lead to a change in any or all of the others, either immediately or in the long run. Thus, developing clearer organizational goals may lead to increased morale and cohesion. But, most frequently, one of these four focal issues is presented as the primary issue that the client system is confronting.

Blake and Mouton offer no explicit reasons for including these four focal issues and not including others. It is difficult to understand, for example, why communications or roles were not included as additional focal issues. Without slighting the importance of the four focal issues identified by Blake and Mouton or arguing against the usefulness of the Consulcube as an integrative device, their focus on these four issues to the exclusion of others is puzzling.

In discussing the four focal issues, Blake and Mouton do note that power and authority concerns are primary in both frequency and importance. Thus, in discussing power and authority as a focal issue, Blake and Mouton note that the consultant must be aware of his or her level of intervention into power and authority problems. If, for example, the consultant is engaged by those having little power—middle-level managers or workers—his or her options will be very different than if the consultant is engaged by those higher up in the power hierarchy. Blake and Mouton note that, in working with persons having less power and experiencing problems with their powerlessness, there is a strong tendency to use acceptant interventions. While such acceptant intervention may, indeed, reduce the emotions that have blocked effective problem solving about the power issues, these issues may not be soluble by those without the power. Rather, some dialogue between the powerful and the powerless may be necessary for any real solution to occur. Thus, while an acceptant intervention may be initially helpful, the consultant must then move to a catalytic one—one that opens up communications between the powerful and the powerless. This shift in the consultant's role requires, however, that the powerful also have confidence in the consultant's skills and appreciation of their interests. But, if the consultant is seen as an agent of the powerless, as too much of an advocate, it may be difficult or impossible for the consultant to make this shift to the catalytic role. If, on the other hand, the consultant fails to serve an acceptant role for the powerless in the first instance, the consultant may develop no credibility with them, with the result that the consultation may never ever begin to make progress. Goodstein and Boyer (1972) report in some detail a consultation with a municipal health department where exactly such a dilemma was encountered.

The most general point made by Blake and Mouton, however, is that the kind of intervention that the consultant may employ —acceptant, catalytic, confrontational, prescriptive, or theory-and-principles-based—may partially be dictated by the nature of the focal issue. Morale and cohesion problems seemingly are best handled by acceptant interventions. Norms and standards concerns seem to be most amenable to catalytic interventions. Power and authority issues seem to respond best to confrontational strategies. Blake and Mouton do not suggest that there are any special applications for either prescriptive or theory-and-principles-based interventions, although they do note that the latter are applicable to the entire range of focal problem. They do note that theory-and-principles-based interventions are unlikely to be successful when there is either a high or low level of affect involved in the situation. Neither apathy nor fanaticism are likely to respond to rational, theoretically derived solutions. In any event, Blake and Mouton are quite clear and explicit—the effectiveness of the consultant is dependent on his or her competence in diagnosing the focal issue and designing an appropriate intervention.

Process Consultation Approaches to Understanding Organizations

In the last chapter we defined process consultation as that approach to consultation that focused on the interpersonal and group interactions by which groups and organizations go about doing their work. Schein (1969), in articulating the notion of process consultation, identified six kinds of human organizational processes that are worthy of special attention by the consultant: (1) communication; (2) member roles and functions; (3) problem solving and decision making; (4) group norms and group growth; (5) leadership and authority; and (6) intergroup cooperation and competition.

Schein notes that these particular processes are somewhat arbitrary on his part but that they do stem from his consultation experience and his understanding of the theoretical and research literature in social psychology, anthropology, and sociology. He especially notes the relevance of the theoretical work of Kurt Lewin (1951); the research on small groups of R. F. Bales (1950); the classical experiments of Lewin, Lippitt, and White (1939) on the effects of different kinds of leadership on group productivity; the work of the NTL Institute for Applied Behavioral Science (formerly the National Training Laboratories) in developing group dynamics training programs or sensitivity training; the research at the Hawthorne Plant of the Western Electric Company (e.g., Roethlisberger and Dickson, 1939) on the importance of "informal" organizations in industry; and the body of psychological research on intergroup relations. Schein thus notes the underlying behavioral-science base for a process approach to consultation.

Schein regards communication as one of the most important and directly accessible of the organizational processes. Who communicates with whom, for how long, what about, how often? These questions are all reasonably answerable by direct observation and by questionnaires or interviews. Further, the pattern of written communication can be analyzed by an examination of the organization's files. Of particular interest is the pattern of communication within staff meetings, which is often where the most important decisions affecting the organization are made. Argyris (1970) uses a careful analysis of the patterns of communication within such meetings, and what they reflect about how important decisions are made, as the primary basis of his consultation work.

What needs to be underscored at this juncture is that the process consultant is not interested in the content of these communications but in the process of communication. Who is not included in the communication net, who speaks but apparently is never heard, whose words seem to have especially heavy impact, who never is allowed to finish his or her thoughts? What are the norms of the organization around communication? Do people wait to be called upon to speak, or is there an open give-and-take? Does one wait for another to finish speaking, or can one interrupt? Can superiors interrupt juniors, or is the reverse permitted? The perceptive consultant does not require much exposure to the work life of the organization before considerable data on these questions and on other aspects of the communicative process of the organization becomes available.

In discussing the functional roles of people in groups Schein makes the important differentiation between task and maintenance functions, as they manifest themselves in group problem-solving situations at staff meetings. First, let us examine the task functions, as described by Schein. In such situations, for the group to make progress there must be some *initiating*. The problem or task must be *identified, alternative solutions* must be proposed, *time parameters* must be set, and so on. To continue the problem solving, various *opinions* need to be given, facts and other *information* need to be addressed, the issues continually need to be *clarified* and *elaborated* to test the quality of the decision toward which the group is moving. Finally there needs to be some attention given to *summarizing* the tentative decisions of the group, and there needs to be *testing for consensus.* All of these task functions must be carried out for effective group decision making or problem solving to occur. In observing a group at work, one of the consultant's tasks might be to identify these processes when they occur and even to note certain regularities in who performs each of these functions.

Not only must each of these task functions be carried out but also some attention must be paid to the interpersonal relationships in the group as they are affected by the work on the task at hand. Maintenance functions are those attempts by members of the group to maintain good interpersonal relations or to repair damaged relationships. Included under maintenance functions are *gatekeeping,* or making sure that all members have an opportunity to participate; *encouraging,* which serves much the same purpose; and *harmonizing* and *compromising,* which tend to smooth over disagreements and disharmony. In addition are *diagnosing, standard setting,* and *standard testing* by which the group suspends task operations and examines its own process, determines how the members are feeling about the group and its mode of operation and, of considerable importance, permits the open airing of problems and conflicts which may have arisen during the task phase. It is these last maintenance functions that almost invariably require the presence of a process consultant. Yet Schein notes that such maintenance roles are essential to the effective use of groups in problem solving and decision making.

Little additional needs to be said at this point about the final four organizational processes enumerated by Schein—problem-solving group norms, leadership, and intergroup relationship. Each of these is certainly an important aspect of organizational life and requires both the understanding and the attention of the organizational consultant.

A Differentiation-Integration Model for Understanding Organizations

Most organizational theorists recognize that one of the most important characteristics of organizations, even the two-person dyad, is the division of labor. It is clearly more efficient if one washes the dishes while the other dries, if there is some differentiation of task and an assignment of each task to a particular individual or group of individuals.

This efficiency becomes even more apparent when one studies complex tasks, like health delivery. One person cannot deliver the same quality health care as a modern hospital. Alone, the person must be admitting clerk, case-history taker, laboratory technician, radiologist, internist, surgeon, nurse, orderly, cook, record keeper, billing clerk, and so on. In a large modern hospital, each of these tasks can be assigned to different people or groups so that expertise can be developed. This specialization also should produce efficiency as well as competence, but efficiency requires coordination of the efforts of each aspect of the system. The larger the organization, the greater the benefits of specialization or differentiation *and* the greater the difficulties of coordination or integration. Thus large size is both the goal and the bane of all organizations as they try to balance the problems of differentiation and integration.

One of the problems is the basis of differentiation. How shall tasks be assigned—on the basis of competence, credentials, seniority, nepotism, gender, race, or by chance? Further, how finely can tasks be differentiated before all challenge is eliminated? How many subunits can an organization tolerate before meaningful integration becomes impossible? Most of the complaints directed against large, complex organizations tend to focus on the breakdown of the integration process—the "snafus" that enrage us when we have been sent to Section B by Section A, only to discover that it may be Section C or even Section A that is the only one that can help us. Yet successful organizations do require adequate differentiation of function and these functions then require integration.

Lawrence and Lorsch (1967), operating from an open-systems model of organizations, have developed an approach to understanding such organizations primarily based upon how they manage the differentiation-integration balance. They note, for example, that the more differentiated the units of an organization become, the more difficult it is to produce integration. As each unit becomes more specialized, it tends to develop its own norms and values—norms and values that are different from other units—thus making integration difficult because of the deep suspicion we have of those who do not share our norms and values. As one example, consider the typical relationship between the university library and the rest of the university community. Parenthetically, it is interesting to note the important function that norms and values play even in a differentiation-integration model.

It was further postulated by Lawrence and Lorsch that the differentiation-integration pattern would not only be affected by the size of the organization but also by the kind of environment in which the organization operates. In stable economic environments, there would be less differentiation than in more turbulent environments because the turbulence would require greater differentiation to meet the constant demand for change and flexibility, especially in those aspects of the organization which were at the boundary with the environment. At the same time, they argued, the greater differentiation would require greater integration; otherwise these environmental pressures would lead to organizational failure.

The research conducted by Lawrence and Lorsch strongly supports their hypotheses. Using industries in three different environmental levels of turbulence, they found that the more successful organization had a structure which enabled it to meet effectively the environmental demands. That is, in stable environments the more successful organizations were less differentiated and thus had less need for integration. The reverse was true in the more changing, turbulent environments, such as in the plastics industry, where the most successful organizations were both more differentiated and more integrated.

Weisbord (1976a), in a highly provocative application of this model to university medical centers, concludes that integration of such institutions is difficult, if not impossible, because the tasks which these institutions attempt to work on are differentiated *within the same person* rather than between persons or groups. In these medical centers a member of the medical faculty is concerned with patient care, teaching, research, and administration rather than having such functions separated into different people. Thus, the managers of such systems who are charged with the task of producing integration are hard pressed to know what to do when the integration is within the individual and operates at his or her whim. One of the clearest implications of Weisbord's analysis is that the differentiation-integration function may indeed be rather different in most human services delivery systems than in the business and industrial world. Both consultants and researchers need to attend to these differences.

Weisbord's Six-Box Model of Understanding Organizations

Operating out of a general open-systems model, Weisbord (1976b) has identified six organizational processes which need to be examined in order to understand an organization fully. The model, presented in Fig. 4.1, is simply an attempt to identify six interrelated processes which can be observed in all organizations and which are not dependent upon any particular theoretical point of view.

As we can note from Fig. 4.1, the organization does exist in the environment and the interaction between the organization and its environment, especially the management of the boundary condi-

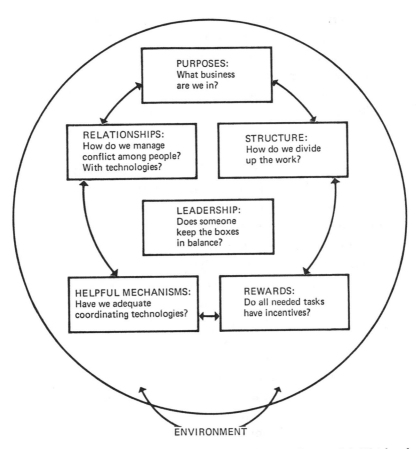

Fig. 4.1 Six-Box Model of Organizational Diagnosis. Source: M. Weisbord. Organizational diagnosis: Six places to look for trouble with or without a theory. *Group and Organization Studies* (1976) 1: 430. Reproduced with permission of M. Weisbord and Organization Research and Development, a division of Block Petrella Associates.

tions, requires close attention. Within the organizational model we should note that there are two aspects of each one of the boxes —the formal system or the work to be done, and the informal system or the process of doing this work. Thus, when we consider *purposes*, we need to investigate both goal clarity (formal) and goal agreement (informal). That is, how clearly do members of the organization see the purposes of the organization and how much commitment is there to the achievement of those goals?

When we examine *structure*, we need to study both the formal table of organization and how the work is actually performed (or is not performed). In studying *relationships* we need to study who deals with whom on what issues and the quality of those relationships. In considering *rewards* (or incentives) we need to examine both the explicit system of salary, wages, bonuses, promotions, and so on and the more implicit psychological rewards of how people feel about a job well done and how much support there is in the system for achievement. In evaluating the *leadership* of the organization, we need to be aware of what the management responsibilities of the leaders are and how well they perform these roles. The formal aspects of *helpful mechanisms* are the budgeting, management information, and planning systems used by the organization, and the informal aspects refer to how these systems may be subverted for other purposes, or not used at all.

What the Six-Box Model provides is a convenient overview of several critical organizational processes and a further subdivision of those into content and process dimensions that can be useful to the organizational consultant as he or she proceeds with an organizational diagnosis. Further, a thorough analysis of an organization based upon this model should provide a consultant with a focus on those organizational aspects which require greater attention in developing an intervention program.

In this chapter we have provided a brief overview of several different ways of thinking about organizations. While open-systems theory is clearly one of these and lies at the core of both the Consulcube and the Six-Box Model, open-systems theory is too broad and general to be of much use in real-life situations. The Consulcube helps provide an overall understanding of the consultation process but the Six-Box Model seems to be the most useful to the actual conduct of organizational consultation and we shall rely most heavily upon it, especially in Chapter 6.

Entry Issues in Organizational Consultation

U p to this point we have considered organizational consultation on a fairly broad basis, focusing our attention on a variety of definitional and conceptual issues. We shall now examine the process in a sequential, orderly fashion, beginning rather naturally with the entry process. It should be clear, however, that most consultations are not orderly and that the stages discussed in this and the following chapters are conveniences of the author.

The Initial Contact

Client systems contact consultants for a variety of reasons. The client has typically identified some problem with which help is required—there is concern with the current personnel selection procedures, something needs to be done about supervisory training, a workshop on effective communications has been suggested, there is some kind of irresolvable "personality conflict" within the organization, and so on. It is rather rare that the client identifies the problem in any systemic fashion, or uses any of the several models of organizational life described in Chapter 4 to describe the issues with which the organization is concerned. Rather, the client system presents "symptoms" that may suggest to the consultant some underlying problem in one or more of the organizational models. One of the early issues of the consultation is to develop a diagnostic strategy for better understanding these underlying problems. How this can be done will be the subject of the *next* chapter, but that there is frequent misidentification of the problem by the client system is one fact of the entry process. One of the important implications of this fact is that consultants need to be wary of what they agree to do during this initial phase.

We have one illustration of how misinformation is presented in the initial contact, and the pitfalls that are caused by this information, in the case reported by Goodstein and Boyer (1972) in which there was the initial request for a "communications workshop." It quickly became apparent that the municipal health department involved was racked by turmoil, that there was a high degree of hostility and suspicion, and that any attempt to conduct such a workshop would have led to open warfare between the Health Commissioner and his supporters on the one hand and his opponents on the other. Indeed, even if the consultants' role had been seen as that of conducting such a workshop, their credibility would have been seriously questioned. Even when the consultants were presented as "diagnosticians and problem solvers," it was difficult to get a hearing from the dissident elements in the organization. The lessons to be learned from such experiences is that consultants need to be presented as neutrally as possible and that they need to agree to very little until there is a clear diagnostic picture.

One point to note is that consultants will frequently be approached on the basis of their presentation of self to the community. If, for instance, we give a lecture to a community group on the importance of open communication in organizations, it is more than likely that we will be asked to visit some organization that sees itself as having a problem in this area. If we have recently been successful in developing a work enrichment program for some organization, then we can expect additional calls for this kind of expertise. While we are clearly not arguing for consultants to hide their expertise, it is important for them to recognize that others will respond to it and that these particular credentials may not be appropriate for the next prospective client.

It was noted earlier that in human service delivery systems, consultants are frequently engaged for some specific task and that more general systemic problems are not identified until much later in the consultation. For example, a consultant may be asked to review the human relations curriculum in a school, or evaluate the recruiting and selection procedures for a municipal police force, or prepare a presentation on behavior modification for the staff of a mental hospital. All of these are legimate professional activities and consultants with such competence should have no hesitation in providing such services and have no qualms about the potential benefits to the client system. But, all too frequently, consultants are told that the human relations curriculum which is under review is not the one that is actually used and the modifications represent some kind of an unworkable compromise between those who "believe in" such programs and those who do not, or that psychometrically sophisticated selection procedures really cannot work in the police department because of covert racism, or that behavior modification programs can never be instituted in the hospital because of the psychological distance between the professional and paraprofessional staff. It is these data that require the consultant's attention for they suggest the need for the particular strategy of process consultation.

If the consultant who initially was engaged as a content specialist now attempts to change his or her role, this often poses difficulty, both for the client system and the consultant. The content specialist is seen as an expert, as someone with the answers, and there tends to be a fair degree of dependency upon such consultants, especially if the consultant has functioned in such an expert role for a lengthy period of time. From the consultant's point of view, he or she has been able to use expert power, demonstrate a high degree of competence, and develop high visibility within the client system. The dependency of the client system often meets some needs of the consultant, thus making these ties difficult to break.

It would indeed be helpful if we could suggest some clear-cut and workable strategies to help both the client and the consultant in disengaging themselves from the initial consultant role of content specialist as they begin to focus on systemic issues, using a process mode. The only one we know of is derived directly from the model of process consultation—talking about these differing expectations. What seems to be of highest importance here is a constant awareness by the professional of the different and special role of the process consultant and a willingness of him or her to reject overtures by the client that he or she resume the more familiar and safer role of the expert. Again, it needs to be reiterated that, since many consultants trained in the helping disciplines are indeed content specialists in the delivery of human services, and they will be working in such delivery systems, there will be innumerable opportunities for them to inadvertently slip out of their process consultant role into that of the content expert. As was noted earlier, every effort should be made to avoid such role confusion as it makes the task of the process consultant just that much more difficult.

Let us now examine in greater detail the actual process of the initial contact and how it is managed. Almost invariably, the initial contact is made by telephone. Someone from another city has recommended that the client call the consultant because of his or her greater accessibility, some colleague who knows the client casually or some other client has recommended the consultant. In discussing initial contacts with groups of consultants it quickly becomes clear that there is no particular system as to who gets called or why they get called.

After some amenities, the client states his perception of the problem and what sort of help he or she thinks is necessary. It is obvious that the client feels that either the existing resources within the organization cannot solve the problem, or that the resources are not already within the system. It should be noted here that many client systems now have internal consultants such as management analysts, development specialists, industrial psychologists, organization development (OD) personnel, and so on. One may wonder why such resources are not used rather than the external consultant, but in all organizations there tend to be process issues that are difficult, if not impossible, for internal people to manage without risking their jobs. Few internal consultants can inform the Emperor that he is naked and that his nakedness is having strong negative consequences for the organization. Indeed, the external consultant usually has not only more courage but more credibility as his perceptions are considered objective and not shaded by personal involvement in the system. We shall return to the matter of internal consultant resources shortly.

While the client does attempt to define the problem in this brief, initial contact, there are frequently uncertainty and puzzlement as well. The client may have adequately identified the problem but does not know how to solve it. For instance, "My chief nurse and the chief of the outpatient department simply won't talk with each other. I've tried to reason with them, but I'm at my wit's end."

Another possibility is that the client may have correctly identified both the problem and the solution, but may lack the strength of conviction and credibility, or the willingness, to take the necessary action. In the case of a community mental health clinic it was clear that one of the satellite operations had been misplaced in an area where the staff was being subjected to continual harassment by the young toughs in the area. Even some of the community residents who had attempted to seek help at the clinic had been bothered by one of these gangs. But closing the clinic would lead to an expression of outrage by the community, so they sought the help of the consultant who could make an objective survey of the effectiveness of the clinic and recommend whether or not it should be continued.

Still another reason for asking for a consultant may result from the perceived weakness of that portion of the client system asking for help in relation to some other part. For instance, the psychology staff at a mental hospital may ask a senior professional to serve as a consultant in its relations with the more powerful psychiatrists. The weaker psychologists may feel that an external, more powerful consultant may help them persuade the psychiatrists of the merits of their position.

Sometimes the client simply states the symptoms in their grossest form—"No one here seems to be getting along," or "This place is hell to work in." There is no serious attempt to define either the problem or the solution. Here the consultant needs to be cautious that the client is not surrendering all responsibility for the problem to the consultant. Even from the earliest contacts the consultant needs to make clear the collaborative nature of the relationship which is expected.

Finally, there are those clients who indicate that there is a problem which they understand only poorly and they wish to have the consultant help in developing diagnostic and intervention strategies. Unfortunately, such ideal clients tend to exist more in texts on organizational consultation than in real life.

Whatever information is offered is superficially transmitted in the initial call and the consultant then is faced with deciding upon the next step. There are two typical next steps, either further discussion at some neutral site, such as lunch at a convenient restaurant, or a visit to the client's base of operation. There are many reasons for preferring the latter. It gives the consultant an opportunity to see the client in his or her natural habitat and to get a glimpse of the work environment. There is much to be learned by seeing the physical location, for example, how much color is used, the quality of the office material, the amount of space given to each person, how people are handled in the reception area, and so on. Steele (1973) has identified a number of fairly specific indices of the physical setting that can be used in understanding the client organizations; one is the obvious difference (or lack of difference) in the size and elegance of offices of persons in the organizational hierarchy. This is immediately observable, even in an initial contact.

But the client often prefers the initial face-to-face meeting on neutral ground. Indeed, it may be that the client is aware of how much may be revealed by inviting the consultant to the home turf. Or perhaps having tentative, exploratory discussion under less formal conditions may be seen as less binding than is a formal meeting "at the office." Perhaps the client may feel that buying lunch for his companion may be a partial repayment for the time and energy that the consultant puts out in this initial contact.

Regardless of where the first face-to-face meeting occurs, the tasks to be accomplished during that meeting are relatively straightforward. First, the client will attempt to clarify further the nature of the problem and the expectation about what might be done. The client will also attempt to learn more about the consultant and his or her background of experience with such problems, and such organizations. Many clients believe that the consultant should have fairly broad experience but also should have had prior consulting experience with an institution similar to the one at hand in order to work effectively in this situation. The consultant must not be defensive about any lack of prior experience or of falsely raising the client's expectation about the many successful years of solving similar problems in similar settings. Rather the consultant should attempt to set the norm of his or her own intervention by being open, nondefensive, and collaborative. Finally, the client will be concerned about the costs of the consultant's services and these will need to be discussed.

Second, the consultant will attempt to characterize what he or she conceives to be an appropriate consultant role, given the problem presented by the client, especially its collaborative aspects. The consultant will attempt to indicate that the client's description of the problem is part of the data base, but the case needs to remain open for further consideration as additional data become available. Communicating this option to the client is frequently difficult as the client is often concerned about sharing some perceived failure with another and experiencing guilt or anxiety about the meeting in progress. The skill with which the consultant handles this issue is often critical to the rest of the consultation process. The consultant needs to serve in both an acceptant and a catalytic role during this meeting. He or she will try to indicate that the role is one of consultant to the organization in some broad sense, not to a particular administrator or subunit. While the consultant may, of course, be engaged to work with a particular part of a larger organization— the out-patient department of a hospital, the personnel section of a community agency, or the psychology department of a university —it is the overall picture that he or she has been hired to examine.

Of special concern is the condition in which the organization is in conflict and the initial contact is made by one of the warring factions. If the consultant is to serve a catalytic role as a neutral third party, it is imperative that the other factions be brought into the negotiation for his or her services as soon as possible. If this is not done, the consultant will be seen as the "hired gun" of the faction that brought him or her into the situation. In the city health department case (Goodstein and Boyer, 1972) mentioned earlier, the consultants were engaged by the Board of Health at the recommendation of the Health Commissioner. When the appointment was announced to the staff of the department who were disenchanted, to say the least, with the commissioner and the board, an anonymous memo was circulated which read, "The workers' council recommends that the staff *not* meet, talk, or give any information to the two new staff psychologists. We recommend that the commissioner and the Board of Health *meet* with these therapists, since the problems in the health department are their problems, not ours." This immediately established friction.

While we have been discussing the initial contacts as part of the entry phase of the consultation process, it needs to be pointed out that the several phases of the process are arbitrary divisions for didactic purposes—there are no clear-cut phases in consultation. What the consultant needs to communicate during the first meeting is that the client has introduced a problem and that the next functional steps are to further evaluate this problem by additional data collection. While any diagnostic evaluation and intervention planning would be premature at this early stage, the need for additional data and for a collaborative stance to both diagnosis and action are the important considerations.

There are several other aspects of the initial face-to-face meeting that may be of concern. The consultant needs to be aware of the negative feelings that the client may have in needing to seek help with an internal problem, and he or she must be careful neither to augment these feelings nor dissipate them by reassuring the client that "all organizations have such problems." As in working with individuals, the consultant needs to be simultaneously acceptant of the client and the client's problems without either magnifying or minimizing them. In this connection it is important that the consultant discuss the client's concerns in straightforward language. This is a special problem when both the client and the consultant come from mental health backgrounds. What might seem to be a use of common jargon may turn out to be miscommunication. It is better to talk in nontechnical language about the systemic problems of the

client rather than in the esoteric language of the helping professions. For example, the organization has problems in dealing with
those in authority, rather than having "Oedipal concerns."

As a seeker of help, the client will often be concerned about
whether or not the consultant can offer a "money-back guarantee."
While it certainly is legitimate to indicate that the consultant has
had previous success in working with client systems experiencing
similar problems, no such guarantee can be offered. It is more
appropriate to deal with the underlying anxiety rather than attempt
to deal with this issue itself. Actually, there are situations in which
the client tests the integrity of the consultant and, if the consultant
does offer come concrete result, the client terminates the negotiation.

What should be accomplished at the initial face-to-face meeting?
Frequently the only outcome of this meeting is an agreement for
both the client and consultant to "think about" some continuing
relationship, with the agreement typically for the client to contact
the consultant about next steps. Sometimes it is more reasonable for
the consultant to check back with the client. There needs to be a
passage of time in which the consultant can determine if there still
is serious thought being given to the utilization of his or her services. Sometimes an initial contact, thought to be fruitless, will be
followed up by a client at a much later date when the consultant is
too busily engaged to take on the job.

The Contract

Usually the client and the consultant can agree to a tentative working contract, or rather two contracts, one formal and the other
informal. There are different ways in which the formal contract is
written, ranging from a formal, legally drafted document with a
variety of written guarantees about not divulging organizational
secrets to an off-hand statement about sending a bill every month,
with no formal or written agreement. Of much more importance is

the informal or psychological contract in which there is agreement about the collaborative nature of the relationship, the initial focus on gathering additional information, and some initial grasp of what process consultation will involve.

As part of the contracting process, some time needs to be set aside to process the work of the consultant-client team to date. This processing of the consultant-client relationship has two purposes. First, it provides for the client an example of how process consultation actually works and, second, it surfaces and hopefully resolves some of the hidden issues that might otherwise interfere with the entry phase of the consultation. To elaborate the first of these points, it will be necessary to the consultant to suggest that such processing is legitimate and timely. "Before we end this meeting and agree to work together, perhaps it is worthwhile for both of us, you as the client and me as the consultant, to talk about how we feel this relationship has gone thus far." Such an opening provides the client with an opportunity to learn how to raise interpersonal issues that have been troublesome by practicing this behavior with the consultant in the receiver role. Or the client may indicate that there was concern that the consultant was seen as too eager to accept the consultation before the situation had been adequately described. Other issues can be raised that would otherwise remain latent, perhaps to come up later when they could be less easily resolved.

Also the consultant can indicate that there was concern about whether or not the client had portrayed the situation as more amenable to change than is really the case, or perhaps that the situation is probably more complex than was described. This initial effort at using confrontational strategies is an excellent diagnostic cue about the willingness of the client to work process issues, to test for openness, nondefensiveness, and a willingness to learn new procedures for working collaboratively on issues. It should be clear that the issues that both the client and the consultant raise in the phase of establishing a contract are real ones, genuine concerns that might have interfered with the relationship in the future. We are not suggesting any role playing here!

One essential part of the informal contract is the agreement for the client and the consultant to process their relationship on some regular basis. While many consultants using this process consultation model attempt to allow time for processing each contact with the client system, there are some critical times when an in-depth processing of the relationship is necessary. Jumping ahead a bit, at the end of the diagnostic phase, after the consultant and the client have agreed upon their joint understanding of the problem and before they begin to develop interventions, such a processing would seem necessary. "How have things gone thus far? Are each of us satisfied with the progress to date? How could we have done this better? Is our work together cost effective?" These are all questions that need to be asked, and answered before the next step is attempted.

What we are suggesting is that, in process consultation, after any major step is completed, the client and the consultant need to process the relationship. This amounts to a renegotiation of the contract at each of the major phases of the process, which is why we have included this discussion at this point. The initial contracting needs to make this norm of recontracting explicit, with the additional proviso that such processing and recontracting can be instigated whenever either party feels the need for it. It further needs to be made explicit that one possible outcome of such recontracting is the decision that the consultation be discontinued. Indeed, many consultants will commit or contract themselves to only one phase of the consultation at a time, thus forcing both themselves and the clients to thoroughly examine their respective satisfactions with the progress to date.

There are, too, a number of more practical matters that need to be considered during the contracting process. Some tentative time frames need to be set, for example, when will various aspects of the consultation be completed and how much of the consultant's time will be required? Also, who else will the consultant be using from outside the client organization? This is an important issue as many university-based consultants regularly involve graduate students in their consulting work in order to teach them these complex skills. Also, will the consultant have access to interorganizational memos, to all levels of the organization, to other relevant data?

One must, as well, explore the role of the person negotiating the contract for the client organization and examine the issues that arise from his or her position. We have already noted some of the issues posed when the consultant is seen as an advocate for one side or another in an organization in conflict, but there are other, more subtle, issues that can arise. Does the personnel director, for instance, engender enough confidence about his or her motives or will the consultant be perceived as yet-another "hatchet man" for some reorganization scheme? Does the fact that the consultant has previously worked with the curriculum group reduce his or her perceived effectiveness with a total school unit? Is the group responsible for bringing the consultant into the system a high-or low-status group? Will the consultant be seen as yet another "wild-eyed" idea of the newly appointed director who has yet to build confidence in his or her judgment? It is incumbent upon the wise consultant to attempt to detect these sorts of concerns through working with the client during the early meetings.

One specific matter that needs to be resolved is who the contact individual is for the consultant. While it can usually be assumed that the person, or persons, involved in the initial contact will maintain the continuing liaison, that is not always the case. The personnel or training director or some internal consultant may make the initial contact and draw the contract, but the agency or institutional director may be the focus of the consultation. Many consultants will not agree to any contract until they have an opportunity to spend some time with the person who will serve as the focus of their work, for such persons are in the position of helping or hindering the entire consultation process.

While we have been discussing the initial contact and the contracting process as single events, it should be noted that we are really discussing a process, and several meetings may be involved as some of the issues discussed above get worked through within the client organization. The entry process and the psychological contract lead the consultant to the point where the nature of the task is clear to both him or her and the client. Further, these early meetings should provide some understanding of the consultant, the procedures which will be used in the consultation, and the underlying values upon which these procedures are based.

Value Dilemmas in Consultation

In Chapter 3 we discussed the values by which consultants who operate through a process mode attempt to work. Briefly, these are humanistic values that place high regard on collaboration, participative management, democracy, the integrity of the individual, and on congruence between individual and organizational goals. But most organizations do not hold to such values. Thus, almost invariably, organizational consultants find that their own values and their client's values differ. What is the impact of these value differences and how do they affect the consulting relationship, especially in the entry phase?

As one extreme example, what should a consultant do if such an organization as the American Nazi Party or the Ku Klux Klan asked for help in becoming more effective? Most consultants, recognizing the gross disparity between their own and their client's values, would simply refuse to consider the job. Some consultants might argue that working within such an organization as a process consultant would, over time, change the character of the system. One might, in turn, argue that there would be an equal chance that the values of the consultant might be changed. But most consultants would agree that an attempt to subvert the goals and values of an organization would be a serious breach of professional ethics. Therefore most consultants, in discussing such hypothetical situations, agree that the most professional and ethical response would be to decline to consult with any organization committed to substantially different values and objectives from the consultant's own.

Yet some value differences, although more subtle, regularly exist between the client and the consultant. Most organizations tend to operate out of either strong task or role orientations. Harrison (1972) identifies *task orientation* as that aimed at the achievement of some high goal. In business and industrial organizations, of course, this goal is to make a financial profit and most organizational values are basic to achieving that particular task. For organizations operating under a task orientation, the consultant is asked to help in increasing productivity. This is to be done either directly, by developing better work procedures, or by eliminating problems such as poor communications or conflict that interfere with productivity.

The *role-oriented* organization is one in which there is strong emphasis on hierarchy and status and all organizational behavior is spelled out by agreements, rules, and procedures—the typical bureaucracy. As we have noted earlier, many organizations in the human service area tend to be role oriented, although there may be some task orientation present as well. But the important point for our consideration is that, regardless of the orientation of the client system, it is almost never one of democratic, participative values. While Harrison does include such a *person orientation* in his typology of organizations, noting that such organizations exist to serve the needs of their members, he points out that few existing ones operate by such an orientation. The fourth orientation in Harrison's typology is *power*, in which the organization attempts to dominate its environment and conquer all opposition. We will return to this typology of organizations in the next chapter as Harrison has provided a useful paper-and-pencil instrument to help identify such ideologies.

The issue here is that the value of orientation of the consultant does differ from that of most organizational clients and, when the difference is not as clear or marked as that of fascistic groups, the response of the consultant tends to be more equivocal. The consultant, for example, may note, as does Harrison (1972, p. 123), that there are important pressures on modern organizations to involve more of a person orientation and the client needs to be exposed to this by the consultant. The problem is that such a response suggests the client has asked for an exemplar of a value position rather than concrete help with fairly specific problems.

Another typical response by consultants when this value dilemma is pointed out is that the consultant's primary role is that of providing valid information to the organization about itself (Argyris, 1970). While this is certainly part of the consultant's role, perhaps even the primary one, what the consultant perceives as valid information will always be shaped by the consultant's values. If, for example, the consultant believes that open communications will make the organization a more effective one, then he or she will "see" the organization's communication through such a perceptual filter. We often are simply not aware of how our values affect our own behavior. If we ask a manager in the client system if he or she discussed some aspect of their work with their subordinates, this very question is value loaded for it implies that such a behavior, even if it had not been performed, should have been considered. By asking such questions on a regular basis, the consultant begins slowly to modify the values of the client organization. All of this, of course, reinforces the underlying point that the commitment to valid information is, in and of itself, a value commitment.

What often happens, however, is that the consultant begins to encounter client resistance engendered by the client's awareness of the value discrepancy. This resistance is evidenced by increasing difficulty in scheduling appointments, by having key persons in the organization "unavailable," by losing access to important data, and so on. This client resistance puts the consultant in the position of having to take personal responsibility for the program that had been collaborative, often trying to wear down the client's resistance by a frontal assault. This, of course, tends to heighten the resistance still further which, in turn, increases the consultant's frustration and sense of failure. This escalation will naturally lead to a discontinuation of the consultant-client relationship with a deep sense of failure on the part of both.

How can this impasse be avoided? How can the consultant approach the client, recognizing that there will always be a value discrepancy leading to some dilemmas in the relationship? While certainly not an easy or a simple answer, the only resolution that we see is to approach the client openly from our earliest contact, clearly articulating our values while recognizing that the client will not immediately understand the implications of our differences for the organization. The working through of the value differences between client and consultant does not occur during the entry phase; it can, and must, begin there. These differences will continue to surface throughout the consulting relationship and the consultant is responsible for being aware of them and for trying to process them in an open and nondefensive fashion. The aware and professional consultant assumes that there are differences in values between himself or herself and the client and that the resolution of these differences will not be complete until the consultation itself is concluded.

Given this position, Bowen (1977) has questioned whether the consultant is ever justified in unilaterally refusing to work with any client system, regardless of the value disparity. Taking the extreme position that even the most authoritarian organization may be in need of help, indeed may be most in need of help, the consultant can provide a valid assessment of the organization and its internal problems. If such an organization were willing to expose itself to the consultant and agreed to work collaboratively at developing better understanding and a plan to change itself into a more effective functioning unit, why should the consultant be unwilling to help? While Bowen does note that such a situation is unlikely to occur in real life, there is one criterion that needs to be considered, one which we are willing to endorse. Any consultant in considering a client's request for services needs not only to consider the internal values of the client but also needs to consider the goods or services that the client organization provides.

If the services or goods that the client provides for the rest of society are regarded by the consultant as important and worthwhile, then there is considerable reason to accept the request for help. To argue that all clients have an equal right to consultant time and energy is to pretend that the values of consultants are not important in determining their effectiveness. It may be unlikely that a consultant committed to pacifism can help create a more effective selective service system or that a consultant convinced that nuclear power is dangerous will be helpful to a public utility planning a new nuclear plant. Since there will always be value differences between clients and consultants about internal issues within the organization, it seems most sensible to assume that the consultant should have some belief in the end-product of the client's efforts if his or her efforts are to have any payoff.

In discussing the value differences between clients and consultants, W.W. Burke informally remarked that his personal criterion for accepting a client was less stringent than that suggested above. If the service or product does no harm and does provide significant employment opportunities that would be lost to the society if the organization failed, then the organization is worthy of consultant help. While this is a somewhat more liberal position than the one advocated above, it does highlight the complexity of this value dilemma.

Diagnosis in Consultation

The consultant has worked through the entry issues discussed in the previous chapter and is now ready to begin the more formal diagnostic process. How can we begin this process?

As we suggested earlier, the consultant needs to set some boundaries on the task before the diagnosis can begin. Are we to study the entire health delivery system, or just the hospital, or just the mental health services, or just the out-patient clinic, or what? We must be concerned with the boundaries of the unit identified as our target, and we must know the focus of our concern early in the process.

Once we have identified this target, we need to understand the subunits that are involved and the several individuals within each of the units. Before we begin any formal data-gathering procedures, however, we also must recognize that our entry into the system, even to collect data, is an intervention that will have consequences. First, we are foreigners to that system and there will be questions, concerns, apprehensions, and so on about what we are doing. While we may have dealt with these issues with the agents responsible for bringing us into the system, there are many others who were not involved in those negotiations who probably have considerable anxiety about us. We must be sensitive to these anxieties and fears and develop strategies for dealing with them directly rather than pretending that they do not exist.

Resistance to Diagnosis

These fears and anxieties surface in a number of different ways and the consultant needs to be aware of the many forms that such resistance can take. One of the frequent issues is one of credential checking. "Where did you get your degree? Have you ever worked with a (health care, school system, mental hospital, or whatever) agency before? Could you give us a brief statement of your theory of organizational consultation, leadership, process versus task, for example?" While these may be legitimate questions, the consultant needs to be aware that the questions will provoke resistance and anxiety.

Those parts of the organization that see the consultant moving onto their "turf" may perceive him or her as a direct threat. One group could be the personnel unit, or the unit responsible for internal human relations activities and/or organizational problem-solving. It is understandable that they should feel it is their failure that the consultant has been brought in to remedy.

A frequently raised question of concern is about the confidentiality of the diagnostic data that will be provided to the consultant. If a member of an organization provides negative data about the organization, will he or she be identified in such a way that will have negative consequences? The consultant needs to provide the necessary reassurances but also needs to note that such questions can be further instances of resistance.

Finally, we need to recognize that all of us are apprehensive about change. We have adapted to the present situation, as bad as it may seem. Any change may be in directions that are less than advantageous to one or another of us personally and we approach with ambivalence those who propose or advocate change. The wise consultant recognizes that there will be a period of testing out in which the resistance and ambivalence about the consultant's role will be a major concern.

Thus, in the municipal health department case previously discussed, we were able to deal with the trust issues raised by the board and the commissioner who brought us into the system (Goodstein and Boyer, 1972) as part of our initial negotiations, but these issues quickly surfaced with even greater intensity among the rank-and-file of the organization. In this case the feelings were very apparent and the climate was such that we could have avoided dealing with the issues, even if we had wished to do so. But sometimes less obvious feelings are involved and these require acceptance, reflection, and clarification by the consultants so that there will not be impairment of the data collection process.

Another point needs to be made here. Data will be collected—questions will be asked, impressions will be gained, concepts will be formulated—and everyone involved will be concerned about what will happen to the data. The question, "Who owns the data?" arises. The process consultation model provides a clear answer to this question. The data and the resultant diagnosis are the joint property of the client system and the consultant. Part of the question-asking is a process of increasing self-awareness on the part of the client system as its members begin to process the kinds of inquiries made by the consultant.

When members of the organization begin to realize that the consultant has asked about goal clarity or goal commitment, about job satisfaction, about the congruence of personal and job satisfactions, and so on, they begin to ask each other, over coffee or in other informal settings, how these questions have been answered. The processing of the questions and the answers in such informal groups initiates a change process that cannot be avoided, even if providing feedback to the client system was not part of the consultant's contract.

But providing feedback to the client system about shared perceptions is an integral part of process consultation. While there are occasions when central figures would like to, and often try to, suppress parts of this feedback, such suppressions can never be totally effective as long as there are opportunities for members of the organization to talk informally with each other. While we shall deal more with the techniques and strategies of feedback in the next chapter, the commitment of the consultant to sharing his or her data with those who have supplied it needs to be underscored at this point. Also, it can be recognized that the consultant can use this commitment to help convince some uneasy participants about the openness of the diagnosis process. That is, the consultant can reassure these people that their data will be made available to the total organization and, at the same time, that the anonymity of every contributor will be guaranteed.

Methods of Data Collection

Once we have identified our target organization, we are ready to begin our formal data collection. There are four general methods of data collection that we need to consider using. One, data can be obtained through *direct observation*. Many consultants initiate their work by spending a day or two simply walking about seeing members of the organization at work, observing staff meetings, or following a complete work process, such as observing a client in a community welfare office as the client moves from the reception process to the termination of the system. Another method is to spend an entire day with one member of the organization, usually some key executive, and observe his or her behavior through the course of that particular day. This process is often called "shadowing."

A second method of data collection is through the analysis of the *written record*. The consultant may examine annual reports, tables of organization, memoranda, job descriptions, enabling legislation, or anything else that might shed light on the organization and how it does its business. One interesting data source is appointment calendars. These provide a convenient record of who gets to see whom, how much time various subgroups have been able to see key managers, and so on. While there are no formal procedures to be used here, the competent consultant can develop a variety of sources of data by using his or her imagination and clinical acumen.

Interviews are the third method of data collection. While many consultants rely fairly exclusively upon interviews to gather data about the organization, this may not always be possible, especially if the portion of the organization to be studied is fairly large. Even in large organizations, however, the consultant will always want to interview the key operating executives and perhaps a sample of other members as well.

The nature of the diagnostic interview will depend upon the type of organizational issues and the general theoretical model of organizational life that the consultant uses. Thus a Tavistock consultant will be more interested in boundary condition management while an open-systems-oriented consultant will be more interested in transformational processes, that is, how the organization changes input to output. But regardless of the orientation of the consultant, there needs to be a high degree of clinical sophistication as the consultant and client interact in the interviews. The consultant needs to be aware of how resistance can block the client's responses, of how nonverbal communications can alter what the client is saying, or perhaps how the client may be trying to influence the consultant to ask a question that will open up some new area that had been closed. We make the point here again that there is no substitute for clinical competence in organizational consultation, any more than there is in medicine, counseling, or clinical psychology.

The fourth method of data collection includes *questionnaires or surveys* of a paper-and-pencil kind that can be used to tap such dimensions as morale, attitudes, values, ideologies, and satisfactions. Not only are there a large number of such instruments commercially available from many of the psychological test publishers but also the research literature on both organizational behavior and organization development report on many, more experimental instruments. Further, the consultant may develop an instrument especially for the particular situation if there are no others available. The major consideration is exactly what sort of information the consultant wishes to develop in order to develop a diagnosis.

As one example of a survey instrument and how it can be used, let us further discuss the Organizational Ideology Scale developed by Harrison (1972) and initially discussed in the preceding chapter. The scale presumes that there are four basic organizational values or ideologies: power, role, task, and person. The questionnaire asks the respondent to rank 15 sets of four statements that give different descriptions or perceptions of the organization. The form, when scored, gives the respondent's overall ranking of these four ideologies, and a mean profile can be constructed for any unit or subunit within the organization.

A consultant recognizing that there is conflict between the research and development section of a social service agency and the rest of the agency might have such a survey completed by the entire organization. The ideology of the research group could then be compared with that of the rest of the agency. If, for example, the research and development section were highly task oriented and the rest of the agency was highly role oriented, the reasons for the intramural conflict would be more apparent. The feeding back of these data to the total organization might require the different segments to examine their values more openly and thus some value reconciliation might be possible. At the very least, the organization will understand the value differences that lie at the core of the problem. It can be noted that a strong reason for using such paper-and-pencil instruments is that they enable the consultant to develop a broader operating base and also give him or her greater credibility as these methods are often seen as more objective than other methods of data collection.

The Inquiry Process

Given that the initial resistance of the total unit is worked through and the several different data sources available, where should the consultant begin the inquiry process? The client has already provided considerable data on his or her perception of the issues that require attention. It is usually useful to begin with some attention to these, even if there are also some data to suggest that the client's own diagnosis is either incomplete or incorrect. There are a number of reasons for following the client's lead, not the least of which is that such behavior strongly indicates to the client that the consultant heard the problem presented and that the consultant is indeed both collaborative and amenable.

In one such consultation, the client indicated that the major concern was one of maintaining the organization's values and culture during a period of major expansion. The organization was humanistic in many ways and, despite its size, had maintained values of interpersonal openness, participative management, and concern about its members, including those at the lowest level. The organization was now involved in a massive expansion and, for the first time, was bringing in senior managers from outside the organization rather than promoting from within as had been previously done. The consultant was initially engaged to help the senior levels of management develop ways of transmitting the organization's values to these new managers and to support these values throughout the organization.

The consultant's first diagnostic task was to determine the accuracy of the client's description of the situation. This was done by in-depth interviews of both old and new managers about their perception of the organization's values and the differences they perceived, both between different managers and between this organization and others with which they had worked. It soon became clear that the senior level managers, both old and new, already shared the organization's humanistic values. In fact, these values had attracted the new managers who were interested in the difference in morale and *esprit* that the values engendered. Further inquiry revealed that a more critical value disparity existed at the level of first-line supervision. All of these supervisors had been recruited from the surroundings area and had little exposure to the organization's values in any systematic fashion. Further, the humanistic values were not widely shared in the other, similar organizations from which these workers had come. Thus the diagnosis was that, in order to maintain the organization's values, more attention had to be paid to the recruitment and training of lower echelon personnel, especially first-line supervision. Before the consultant's intervention, these individuals had been selected primarily for their technical expertise and little was done in the way of supervisory training, especially in the clarification of values. While the client had correctly diagnosed the *need* in this case, the analysis of the underlying *problem* led to a rather different course of action than might originally have been anticipated.

The Six Boxes Revisited

In Weisbord's (1976b) diagnostic model of organizational consulta-tion, he identifies six interrelated organizational processes that need to be examined by the consultant during the diagnostic phase of the intervention. While we briefly described this Six-Box Model in Chapter 4, it would seem appropriate to study it in some detail here as it has proven to be a useful approach in our diagnostic experi-ence. One general point that Weisbord makes is that the consultant must avoid seeing failures of these organizational process issues, that is, the blockage of important organizational work, as primarily the function of personality factors, although they might be por-trayed as such initially.

For instance, we have noted that there tends to be little con-frontation in human services organizations. Conflicts are more like-ly to be "swept under the rug" than directly faced. Such conflict management strategies need to be seen as reflecting the norms and values of such organizations rather than personal inadequacy of organizational members. Granted that individuals might select careers in such organizations because the positions meet some personal needs, there are no organizational supports for confronta-tion and the member who tries to change such norms will not find this an easy task. Indeed, when we find such confronting indi-viduals in human service organizations, we often have a bad "fit" between the individual and the organization and neither party may find the relationship very satisfying.

While one can start the organizational diagnosis at any of the six boxes, Weisbord notes that they are all interconnected and, regard-less of where one starts, all will be examined in some detail even-tually. Because it is a sensible place to begin, let us start our discus-sion with *purposes,* or goals. As we noted earlier, there are two critical aspects of goals—goal clarity and goal commitment.

In contrast with business and industrial organizations, human ser-vice delivery systems generally have more ambiguous and diffuse goals. While there may be agreement that the goal is to provide "quality" education, health care, or other human services, there tends to be little or no agreement about how these goals are to be achieved in behavioral terms. The goals are so broad that each member defines them in a personal way. Is quality education teaching children basic skills or developing them as social beings, or some combination of these? Since neither educational leaders nor experts can agree on such matters, it should not be surprising that the teachers at Hilltop School, for example, have little goal clarity and even less goal commitment. And the same is largely true in many of the other human service areas.

Such poorly articulated goals lead to increased anxiety and stress within the members of the various organizations, with no balancing norm of open and continuing dialogue that might lead to some greater goal clarity and anxiety reduction. Rather, since these different goals usually have high value commitments on the part of those who hold them, persons who do not share one's behavioral definition of "quality" service are seen negatively and to be avoided or proselytized. One of the important functions that a diagnosis can serve is to bring these differing goal definitions to the surface, together with their underlying values, so that some dialogue may be possible.

But, as Weisbord notes, in such systems the competition often is so strong and the necessary interdependence of persons so low that the members of these organizations resist efforts to clarify goals in order to maintain their autonomy. The consultant entering such systems should note, however, that any conflict, internal or external, is quite covert and will be immediately denied when its presence is suggested.

Another aspect of the goal clarity involves the organization's relationship with the environment in which it lives. Does this agency deliver services that society values and is happy to pay for? The clarity of the agency's goals, as expressed in its behavior as well as in its formal policy statements, clearly affects how the agency is valued by the rest of society. That educators cannot agree on the purposes of schooling, that health services deliverers seem indifferent to human suffering, or that welfare agencies seem powerless to interfere with child abuse all suggest to the public at large that such systems do not have clear goals and thus are not worthy of unequivocal support. Much of the recent work to make such agencies more responsive to public needs is an effort to sharpen goal clarity.

But there is another aspect of the relationship between human services and the surrounding society that is more difficult to modify. Many human service agencies deal with those segments of our society that are held in low regard—the poor, the handicapped, the mentally disturbed, the criminal—and while there is some recognition that services need to be provided to such groups, the support for such services is grudging at best. The lack of societal support for the goals of such service agencies does have its implications for goal commitment within these agencies, further diffusing and diminishing goal commitment among agency staff. Without intervening on a broad social-system level, it is unclear that the organizational consultant can do much to change the fit between these agencies and the society at large. But an awareness of such matters is necessary, as disconcerting as it may be. The low regard with which these tasks are regarded and the grudging societal support given to the persons who work at them—welfare workers, mental hospital aides, prison guards, and so on—produces in them a fair degree of cynicism and a low degree of commitment, even when there is some goal clarity.

The foregoing examples are suggestions of goal issues that may otherwise escape attention and cautions the need for them to be exercised. The organizational consultant needs to examine the written records, interview organizational members, study the relationship between the organization and the environment through a review of the media coverage, or do whatever else is necessary to develop a clarity of perception about the purposes of the organization which is the target of the intervention.

Structure is the second of Weisbord's six boxes. The implicit assumption is that the structure or separation of function is developed to help the organization achieve its goals but this is not always the case, especially when the goals are not clear. There are three major ways in which organizations establish structure: (1) by function, so that experts can work collectively together (thus we have departments of psychiatry, schools of social work, colleges of education, and so on); (2) by product, project, or program, where the task requires the collaboration of different specialists or experts (therefore we have outpatient clinics, intensive care units, interdisciplinary teams, etc.); and (3) some combination of (1) and (2) in which everybody has two bases of operation.

Each of these approaches to structure has both special advantages and special problems. The functional organization enhances the division of labor or differentiation of the organization, and facilitates the development of special skills among its members. But it also enhances competition between functional units so that different departments or sections compete for scarce resources without any regard to the valid needs of other units. Such functional organizations require strong leadership to control this competition and produce some integration of purpose. Functional organizations develop strong loyalties to their separate subunits and are quite stable, thus functioning best in stable environments where high levels of competence are necessary. Colleges and universities are prime examples of functional organizations.

Product, project, or program organizations are, by definition, task oriented and thus are more responsive to a changing environment. Usually the program team is internally adequate to deal with the assigned task and thus has little to do with other teams, cutting down on intergroup conflict. The high task orientation, however, prevents the development of in-depth competence and the high task demands can lead to staff "burn-out" and intragroup conflict. These problems are frequently noted in such task-oriented, interdisciplinary services as drug-abuse control agencies, emergency hotlines, and other crisis-oriented programs.

In order to maximize the advantages and minimize the disadvantages of the function and the program approach, the mixed or *matrix* model has been developed. In this model, which was developed in the high-technology industries in electronics and aerospace, every person has two bases—functional and program. One is both a member of the social work staff and the outpatient clinic, the surgery faculty and the emergency room staff, the psychology group and the ward staff, for example. But, in the matrix model one not only has two homes but two supervisors, and the messages one receives under this model may be different, even contradictory. Ambiguity is high in this model and one can feel that loyalty is difficult to develop and maintain. But the matrix model does provide greater flexibility than either of the other two, and new program teams can be developed across functional areas as needs develop, just as others can be eliminated as tasks are completed. Leadership in this model needs to be strong as there is high conflict over the ambiguity of roles.

In diagnosing the structure, the consultant needs to check carefully on the congruence between it and the goals of the organization. In working with one academic psychology department it was noted that there were three graduate programs offered in the department—experimental, social, and clinical psychology. Course schedules were developed by the three program faculties who gave highest priority to their graduate offerings—this was the function that the structure was intended to serve. Undergraduate course offerings were strictly an afterthought and there was much discontent with the undergraduate program on the part of the students and the college dean. But the structure gave such a low priority to the development of undergraduate teaching that one could conclude that the graduate programs were the primary, if not the sole, reason for the department's existence. For a diagnosis, the consultant needs to attend to what the structure tells about the goals of the organization and how the structure is actually used to help or hinder the accomplishment of work.

The third organizational process in Weisbord's scheme is *interrelationships*. He notes three kinds of relationships that are worthy of study: (1) interpersonal, between peers and between subordinates and superiors; (2) intergroup, between subunits of the organization; and (3) interactive, between workers and technology, or between people and the system or the equipment. One important contribution that Weisbord makes is in noting that there are many work situations in which there is low interdependence between people or units and there is no real need for harmonious or close relationships, either between the people as individuals or between units or groups. Nevertheless there is a strong norm in our society, and it is especially powerful in the human service area, that people should "get along." As a result, there is much forced collaboration that does little to enhance the proper work of the organization. The diagnosis and examination of this issue are clearly important functions of a consultant.

At the same time, of course, there is work that can only be done collaboratively. Curriculum building, long-term planning, and evaluation of organizational adequacy are several examples of situations where collaboration is necessary even where there are low interdependence requirements. At such times, "good" relationships are necessary, both on an interpersonal and intergroup basis.

Another societal norm that is especially strong in the human service area is that conflict is always bad, either interpersonal conflict or intergroup conflict. Weisbord notes that there are certain built-in conflicts in the industrial sector, such as between sales and production, which if well and openly managed can be both legitimate and functional for the organization because each unit needs to see things differently in order to accomplish its own task. We would add that the same is true in human services where we have the conflict be-

tween academic freedom and curriculum planning or between sur-
geons and internists, and so on.

The central issue here is not whether there is conflict, but rather
how the conflict is managed. If there is managed confrontation,
where people can openly argue for what they believe in and have
the opportunity to present both their data and their values, then
such differences can facilitate the organization's reaching its goals.
On the other hand, where there is manipulation, compromising just
to settle things, smoothing over, forcing of solutions by those in
authority, or other ineffective modes of conflict management, then
the organizational consequences will most likely be negative.

The fourth Weisbord's boxes is *rewards*, or whether the organization regularly provides opportunities for growth, responsibility,
and achievement for its members. Weisbord notes that both the research data and the theorizing of such motivational analysts as
Abraham Maslow (1954) and Frederick Herzberg (Herzberg et al.,
1959) clearly suggest that such rewards cannot be solely financial.
Rather, salary and other financial benefits are rewards only when
offered in clear recognition of important work that is congruent
with organizational goals. But in most human service delivery
systems the goals are not clear, managers have difficulty in deciding
whether or not the contributions of staff facilitate the goals, and,
further, see themselves as unable to provide rewards because of the
limitations of the bureaucratic system in which they find themselves. Thus, most workers in the human services area feel that
their efforts are unrewarded, and this has very severe negative
consequences on performance.

The failure of the motivational system is promoted by the
informal norms of the system which are to show little or no initia-
tive, to hide behind rules and regulations in order to avoid responsibility, to put in time rather than accomplish work, and to maintain as low a profile as possible. While there are similar, informal
norms in industrial systems that set performance standards and dis-

courage rate breaking, they do seem to be more all-pervasive and disabling in the public and third sectors.

Clearly one of the tasks of the consultant is to identify how members of the organization perceive the reinforcement schedule of the organization and how this differs from that which is publicly described. What are the payoffs for doing your job well? What are the sanctions against "goofing off"? What are the limits for not performing? How much risk can people take in doing their work? All of these are important questions for which the consultant can and must find answers for his or her diagnosis.

Leadership is the fifth of Weisbord's six boxes. Much has been written on leadership and there is a variety of different systems for categorizing leadership style. Stogdill (1974) has provided a comprehensive review of the research literature on leadership covering over three decades.

Many approaches to leadership are based upon the pioneering work of Lewin, Lippitt, and White (1939). The most common interpretation of their work is that there is a single continuum of leadership behavior ranging from an employee- or people-centered approach at one end and a production or task approach at the other end. This continuum is sometimes seen as ranging from subordinate to boss centered, depending on how much authority is delegated or subordinated to others. The implicit assumption is that the authoritarian leader is always interested in the task and the democratic leader in people, a dubious assumption at best.

The work of Blake and Mouton (1964) in developing the Managerial Grid takes the position that concern with people and production are independent variables and that the truly effective leader is equally concerned with both people and task. On the grid, leaders are evaluated separately for these concerns on two independent scales on a 1–9 rating system with a rating of 9 representing the strongest level of concern. Thus, a 9,9 leader is one with maximum concern for both his people and for accomplishing the task. A 9,1 leader is one with a maximum concern for task and little or no concern for people while a 1,9 leader is one concerned only with people with no concern for getting the job done. Of course a variety of intermediate patterns are also possible using the grid.

Fiedler (1967), however, has concluded that most leaders are either task or people oriented and that both styles are somewhat resistant to change. Since the effectiveness of either of these styles depends primarily upon the situation and neither style is always effective, Fielder recommends the choosing of leaders according to the nature of the task or of changing the task to fit the leader's style. Thus he suggests a "contingency" approach to leadership.

While Weisbord notes that this contingency approach is limited because we often do not know very much about the nature of the organization's task, this is less true in public and third sector organizations. Here the interpersonal skills of the leader in smoothing over conflict, dealing with the anxieties of personnel, and patching up differences help the organization survive but do little to clarify goals and move the organization to achieve these goals. As we noted in Chapter 1, open confrontation is rather studiously avoided in these nonindustrial organizations and thus two of the central functions of leadership—to define, embody, and defend purposes, and to manage conflict effectively—are never performed.

In general, the leadership task is to monitor the operations of the other five of Weisbord's boxes. Successful leaders need both a clear recognition of their roles and the ability to communicate an understanding of and competence in executing this monitoring function. The organizational consultant needs to examine how well these leadership functions are being performed and how they are being perceived by others in the organization.

The last of Weisbord's boxes is *helpful mechanisms*, those informal devices developed to facilitate intraorganization understanding and to help bind the individual members into a cohesive unit. Included are such devices as memo distributions, meeting rooms, bulletin boards, reports at staff meetings, and informal get-togethers.

Weisbord notes that there are four formal organizational processes that require helpful mechanisms in order to function effectively—planning, budgeting, control, and measurement. It is readily apparent that most organizations in the nonindustrial world have either very poor helpful mechanisms for such processes, or none at all. Sometimes they are badly used, causing informal "process" problems with people feeling left-out or mistreated. Educational institutions, for example, have considerable difficulty in planning—how many children will be attending which schools and how shall we plan our building and staffing program to meet expected needs? Rarely are there in-depth planning studies carried out to answer such questions and, even if they were conducted, all too often the planning process is a political rather than a rational one. The organizational consultant needs to look at the organization's helpful mechanisms, as well as the planning, budgeting, control, and measurement processes, in order to identify how helpful these mechanisms are, rather than how helpful they were intended to be.

Finally Weisbord makes the point that each of the six boxes can be examined on three levels and these levels will help target the appropriate interventions: (1) Does the organization have environmental support? Environmental support is essential if the organization is to thrive and prosper. Even the most smoothly functioning organization cannot be helped if it is not seen by the surrounding society as worthy of support. Little would be gained by an in-depth analysis. (2) Does the organization's structure fit its goals and purposes? A community mental health agency that does not structurally involve active community input needs work on this level rather than on the interpersonal or group level. An out-patient clinic that systematically places all requests for its services on a six-month waiting list needs to be examined with the focus on why this occurs rather than on problems based on personality issues. While personal or interpersonal issues may help explain the failure to provide services, the central focus of the consultant's work needs to be on understanding all the reasons for the failure. (3) Do the organization's norms support its intent? If the nature of the task to be performed is collaborative, like research and development, are the norms for sharing and openness or are they for suspiciousness and guardedness? If the intent is to provide some human service, are the norms for dealing with clients to be caring and interested or cool and bureaucratic? In other words, does the informal system coincide with the formal one?

From this overview of Weisbord's diagnostic model, we hopefully have a better idea of how we can proceed with an organizational diagnosis. It is important to reiterate that any questions about any of the six boxes will yield potentially useful information about the system. What is needed is the understanding and clinical skill to follow up these questions until each of the six boxes is examined.

The Role of Diagnosis

Perhaps the most articulate statement on the role of diagnosis in the consulting process is that provided by Chris Argyris (1970). He persuasively argues that there are three primary tasks for the consultant: (1) the development of valid and useful information; (2) helping the client understand the free choices that are open to him or her; and (3) facilitating internal commitment to change.

Of these three diagnostic tasks, the development of valid and useful information is obviously the most critical. By valid information, Argyris means a description of those factors that have created the problem(s) that the client system is experiencing, and the interrelationships among these factors.

The validity of the information can be verified by having several, independent diagnoses and checking for the degree of similarity of the outcomes. A second check is to test the predictions of the diagnosis by varying the conditions described. Thus, we could increase the organization's internal communications and actually see if an improvement in goal clarity followed. A third check would be to vary the several factors involved in the diagnosis in some system- atic fashion and determine the degree of change. Obviously, the known effects of experimenter bias need to be guarded against in such checking procedures.

What if the consultant and the client are able to arrive at valid and useful information—a successful diagnosis? Then the client is provided with a clear and free set of choices about alternative courses of action. The client can continue in his or her present course, recognizing the consequences, both positive and negative. Or, he or she can have a number of alternatives clearly sketched out—aspects of the system which can be changed—and the pro- jected trade-offs for each of these alternatives. In other words, the consultant has provided the client with data, including short- and long-term consequences of a number of different courses of action. It is then the responsibility of the client, with the help of the consultant, to think and feel through those course of action to find which best fit the organization's goals and purposes.

This heavy emphasis on diagnosis may strike some readers as an undesirable reliance on some "medical model" of intervention. Much of the current disfavor with which the medical model is viewed stems not from any intrinsic limitation of the model but, rather, from the inappropriate way in which the model has been applied. The best use of the medical model is, as Argyris says, when the consultant—organizational or medical—is more skilled than the client in both data collection and data analysis. The data is collaboratively collected and the resulting diagnosis is offered to the client as suggesting alternative courses of action with their respec- tive consequences. What has happened in the perversions of this model is that the consultant usurps the choice of the client and makes the decision that is "best" for the client. Good consultants, regardless of the level of their intervention, always leave the choice to the client.

Finally, the Argyris model on intervention focuses on the need for strong commitment throughout the organization to the understanding of the diagnosis and the choice of which alternative to pursue. The chosen plan needs to be "owned" by the organization as a whole if it is to be successfully implemented. The final choice needs to be seen by almost every member of the organization as meeting some of his or her needs and therefore there being some degree of individual commitment to the execution of the plan. Hopefully, the strong collaborative norm established by the consultant throughout the course of the diagnosis makes such an internal commitment more likely than it was earlier.

In concluding this chapter it should be noted that diagnosis is a process rather than a product. The organization will change inevitably during the time of the intervention and the very process of diagnosis will indeed further these changes. All human diagnoses illustrate the Heisenberg Uncertainty Principle and perhaps this is particularly true of organizational diagnosis. The notion that the observation and measurement of a phenomenon changes the nature of what is being observed gets intensified in organization life where rumors, misunderstandings, and so on get communicated from member to member.

Thus a diagnosis, regardless of how thorough or careful, is a snapshot of the organization frozen at a moment in time. While we may take repeated snapshots, by the time they are developed and printed, the organism or the organization has already changed. Thus diagnosis is best understood as a process and one that needs to be continued over time. There are clear implications of this notion to which we will return in Chapter 8.

Interventions in Consultation

Diagnosis as Part of Intervention

Interventions, or planned-change strategies, are the next phase of the consultation process. But, before we examine interventions, two important points need to be made. First, as we mentioned in the previous chapter, the diagnosis or, more properly, the diagnostic phase is itself an intervention.

Depending upon the experience of the client system with consultants in the past and on how effectively the consultants were able to deal with the trust issues during the entry and diagnostic phases, the end-product of the consultant's work may be regarded with anything from keen anticipation to anger and even the disillusionment that the serious problems of the system must be subjected to yet another study. Of course, all the intermediate points along this continuum of reactions can also be found. As we have stated before, the point that should be understood here is that the convenient division of the consultation process into neat phases is useful to textbook writers and other analysts but, from the client's point of view, once the consultant enters the scene, the intervention process has begun.

The second important point to note is that the diagnosis, if properly done, ought to identify the next steps clearly. As Argyris (1970) and others have noted, the diagnosis, in addition to providing valid information to the client, also ought to provide an awareness of alternatives and the consequences of these alternatives. Hopefully, in some collaborative fashion, the client and consultant will begin to develop the alternative that best solves the client's problem(s), according to the client's own value system and priorities.

Perhaps an example from real life would be helpful to illustrate this point. Consultation help was requested by the personnel director of a large scientific consortium. One of the organization's research laboratories was doing poorly. A new manager, Mark, had been appointed about ten months earlier to replace the old curmudgeon who had run the lab for more than 20 years. Mark, a doctoral-level, internationally famous research chemist was having trouble in defining his role as the lab manager, at least according to the personnel director. Parenthetically, it should be noted that the belief that technical competence leads to managerial success is prevalent throughout the managerial world, despite all the evidence to the contrary.

During Mark's brief tenure as manager, the lab had overspent its budget by almost $2,000,000, had failed to complete any of its targeted projects, had lost several key scientists to other organizations, and morale was at an all-time low. Direct observation and interviews by the consultant confirmed this last fact. In talking with Mark, it became clear that he had very little idea of a manager's role. He knew that he neither could nor wanted to behave as his predecessor had, but he had no clear behavioral alternatives. He was reluctant to share his ideas about how work should be done, to set limits for other people, or to embody the purposes of the unit. His failure to provide leadership had led to a reduction in goal clarity, competitiveness rather than cooperation between the lab's subunits, poor relationships on both an interpersonal and group level, and a high degree of frustration. The diagnosis was quite clear—a failure of leadership.

In feeding back these data to Mark and the personnel director, several alternatives established themselves. Mark could relinquish his managerial role (or be fired), the organization could be reorganized with Mark's task sharply reduced in scope, or Mark could be helped to learn managerial skills. For a number of reasons, the latter was the course chosen. The consultant, who by this time had a close working relationship with Mark, agreed to work as Mark's coach and teacher. They agreed to work two days a week together, with the consultant "shadowing" all of Mark's managerial work during that time. Ten minutes out of every hour would be devoted to "time out" when Mark and the consultant would process how Mark had handled that particular situation. The consultant would ask Mark why he had chosen the course that he had, what alternatives had occurred to him, what he saw as the consequences of these various actions, and so on. In addition, Mark was given a series of books on professional management and, later in the consulting relationship, he attended a human-relations-oriented (sensitivity training) managerial workshop for a week.

In this case, the clarity of the diagnosis—a leadership vacuum—led to the intervention strategy in a fairly straight-forward fashion. Something had to be done, and quickly, to resolve the problem. The alternatives were fairly obvious and one was chosen. Consultation assistance was available to help implement the change strategy and continual follow-up could be provided. While all of these aspects cannot always be built into a consultation, this is the approach to intervention that we should like to be able to follow in our consulting efforts.

We previously noted that diagnosis is a continuous process—the development of working hypotheses and searching for confirming or nonconfirming data. This does not end with the intervention phase. Rather, we continually monitor the impact of our intervention and consider how our plans need to be modified, elaborated, or otherwise changed to meet our goals for effective organizational change.

Planning the Intervention

In planning any organizational change, the consultant must be aware of the strong tendency of humans to resist change on both the individual and organizational level. Consultants are often surprised to find such resistance, particularly when it appears that the individual or organization is suffering or otherwise clearly experiencing difficulties.

But even in those situations where pain may be experienced, there may be some rewards that more than offset the pain. On an individual level, the secondary gain or reinforcing properties of some psychological disorders has been well known. On the organizational level, there always will be some individuals who are having their needs met in the present situation and recognize that, for them, any change will be for the worst. Such individuals can become foci of resistance. But, since they require the support of others, they must make their appeal on a broader base than losing known rewards.

Instead of focusing on the cost of change to themselves, such individuals can use any number of other reasons for resisting change and recruiting others to join opposition to changes proposed. Most organizations have a degree of pride in whatever they do and any change proposed can be characterized as a criticism of the organization and its mode of operation. "Who are these out-siders and what do they know about (providing health care, teach-ing kids, helping the poor, and so on)?" Organizational pride also leads to the rejection of outside advice, even from expert, highly paid consultants. The fact that the change was "not invented here" intensifies resistance to that change. This notion helps explain van de Vall's (1975) finding that action research completed by internal consultants had greater impact than that done by external con-sultants.

Further, accepting or supporting any change is often seen as admitting a weakness, especially if the change is promoted by an outsider. If we recognize our own limitations and attempt to devel-op our own remedy, it is less onerous than if outsiders are in-volved. Also, change involves some new behaviors, some new modes of operation. There is almost always a period of awkward-ness when the new behaviors are not quite integrated into our response system and when there needs to be both a willingness to continue with the experiment and support for the attempt. In work-ing with a group of physicians who themselves had been serving as external consultants, and doing poorly at it—hence the request for consultation—a workshop was conducted to help them better understand their "presentation of self" and the reactions that their entry into the client system evoked. It soon became clear, through the use of videotape feedback, that they came across as formal, judgmental, and authoritarian. When, however, they attempted to practice being informal, nonjudgmental, and open, they were un-comfortable and stiff. It took several days of fairly intensive prac-tice and support from each other before there were any signs of behavioral changes that might transfer to the actual consulting task. They also verbalized their fear of failure in their new styles and how difficult such a failure would be to accept. If they failed in their old style, they at least knew how to deal with that.

Consultants, in designing and planning interventions in organiza-tions, need to be aware of the forces against change and plan their change strategy accordingly. Just as there are individuals and groups within any organization that will oppose the planned change, there will be those who support it. The consultant needs to identify both of these groups and then make some determination of the impact of both the opposition and the support. If the opponents are among the more powerful members of the organization, then their opposition will be very significant. But, regardless of their relative power, an awareness is necessary of the existence of these countervalent forces and how they might polarize the organization over time.

While one might argue that the evaluation of the readiness for change is part of the diagnostic phase of the consultation process, the emphasis here is on the reactions to different change strategies and where they might be introduced. Hopefully, the consultant has clarified the client's expectations about the change process in general and about the kind and amount of work that needs to be done for change to occur during the entry and diagnostic phases. It now needs to be done again as the intervention plans crystallize.

In almost all organizations there will be differential readiness among members of subunits to attempt change either because of their distress experienced, their openness of to new experience, the relative cost to them of a failure, or some other reason.

One possible alternative is to use the most "ready" of the subunits as the initial target of whatever interventions are planned. Lippitt, Watson, and Westley (1958) suggest that there are two important criteria to use in selecting which subunit is to be the target of the initial intervention, namely, accessibility and linkage. Accessibility means that the subunit is psychologically open to the consultant's intervention *and* that there is a high likelihood that the intervention will be successful. The unit which is in the most pain or difficulty might be the most open, but might not have adequate resources to be able to profit from the intervention. Linkage refers to the likelihood that the positive consequences of any successful intervention will be communicated to other subunits, increasing the possibility of accessibility in other subunits. The centrality and power of the subunit in the organization are important variables in this linkage function. Clearly, these criteria need to be carefully considered in planning an intervention.

A Typology of Organizational Interventions

In Chapter 3 we introduced the term *Organization Development*, or OD, to categorize those planned change efforts aimed at organizations. When the term OD was initially used some years ago, it referred rather exclusively to those interventions in which process consultation was the primary vehicle for facilitating the change, and we would like to maintain that distinction. However, OD now refers to the methods "for facilitating change and development in people (e.g., styles, values, skills), in technology (e.g., greater simplicity, compexity), and in organizational processes and structures (e.g., relationships, roles)" (Friedlander and Brown, 1974, p. 314). While the goals of OD remain general humanization of organizations through an optimizing of process or task or some combination of these, there is no longer any single technology, approach, or method by which such goals are to be achieved.

Much has now been written on OD and there is a variety of ways in which OD interventions can be classified or categorized. For example, Bennis (1969), French and Bell (1973), and Friedlander and Brown (1974) have each presented their schemes. Bennis' is of interest now primarily for historical reasons and to see how the technology of planned change has developed in the past two decades. Table 7.1 presents an adaptation of the two-by-two table developed by French and Bell (1973, p. 106). This table makes the important distinction between task versus process issues as the focus of the intervention and whether the individual or the organization is the target of the intervention. Many workers in this area, however, would regard many of the individually focused interven-

Table 7.1   OD Interventions Classified by Focus and Target Issue

| | | Target | |
		Individual	Organization
Focus	Task	Formal education-technical, administrative (e.g., budgeting, operations research, etc.) or personal (public speaking, writing, etc.) skills Preparing or revising job description Career planning	Technostructural changes Role negotiation, especially about task assignment Formal (survey) feedback, especially about task and accomplishment
	Process	Coaching or counseling Participation in sensitivity training with strangers rather than colleagues Life planning Training in group dynamics, OD, and other process skills	Team building, within and between units Participation in sensitivity training with other organizational members Formal (survey) feedback, especially about morale, interpersonal relationships, and other process concerns

Adapted from W.L. French and C.H. Bell's *Organization Development.* Englewood Cliffs, N.J.: Prentice-Hall, 1973, p. 106.

tions not as OD interventions, but rather as Management Development (MD). As we noted earlier in Chapter 3, while MD may have consequences for organizational effectiveness, it may be better to restrict the concept of OD to those interventions which directly attack organizational issues.

Since Friedlander and Brown (1974) regard structure and process as the core concepts of organizational theory in systems terms, their conceptualization of OD rests on these two concepts, without attempting to consider whether the target of the intervention may be an individual or a group. It should be clear that, even when the focus of an OD intervention is an individual, such as in coaching, the focus of such coaching is on that person's behavior in organizationally relevant situations.

More specifically, Friendlander and Brown argue for changes that focus on both the technology and the structure or on the people and their interactions. They aptly point out that there is now ample evidence that efforts to change the technology through such techniques as industrial engineering, operations research, or scientific management, or to change the structure through simple, rationally derived reorganizational plans, or to change the people through the use of better selection techniques, encounter groups with strangers, or formal training have failed in the main. Rather, they argue for interventions that take into account the simultaneous interaction of technology of the organization and its structure—the technostructural—or the people in the organization and their interactions—the human "processual" or process. Let us examine a variety of interventions under these two rubrics.

Technostructural Interventions

Technostructural interventions are those change efforts which attempt to change simultaneously the task methods (technology) and the roles, relationships, and other task assignments (structure) of the organization. Such efforts focus at the same time on the work content and methods and the sets of relationships among the persons who do the job. For instance, consider the traditional state mental hospital with patients housed in wards, depending upon the nature of their disturbance—acute, intensive treatment, chronic, children and adolescent, and so on. Each ward is managed by a psychiatrist with most of the other clinical services centralized in an administrative building. The ward psychiatrist must request the social work service or the psychologists to provide service to the patients on the ward and these requests are typically handled as received. The patients at discharge are assigned to the out-patient clinic at the hospital which has as little as possible to do with the in-patien care.

Now suppose that we wished to change that system so that the wards were based on the geographical areas from which patients had come and each such ward had a complete team of mental health professionals and paraprofessionals. The obvious idea underlying such a change is that better care can be provided to the patients and also support systems among neighbors can be developed. Further, these geographicallly oriented wards could have close and continuing relationships with the community mental health centers back in these communities so that the aftercare provided would build upon the treatment the patient had received in the hospital. Such a series of changes represents a technostructural intervention as it simultaneously changes the technology and the structure of the work.

Such a change involves having the mental health professionals now deal with a wider range of patients than they had previously, thus changing the technology of their jobs; and the creation of ward teams in place of the independent, professionally oriented services obviously changes the nature of the relationships among the workers. In this connection, it should be noted that such massive technostructural interventions can arouse strong resistance among those involved for all the reasons previously discussed and can easily fail if there is no attention paid to the human processes involved in creating such changes. Thus, many times an intervention may require both technostructural and process elements.

The work of the Tavistock Institute mentioned previously in Chapter 4 (Rice, 1958, 1963, 1969) has most recently focused on such technostructural issues, as they involve the management of the internal boundary conditions within the organization. Further, how these internal boundary conditions are managed has clear implications for the management of the external boundary conditions. In the case of the mental hospital, the internal restructuring of the wards on a geographical basis changes the relationship between the hospital and the community in which the hospital operates. The internal changes should provide some reduction of the barriers between the hospital and the community and permit a closer and more productive relationship.

Friedlander and Brown note that there are three major kinds of technostructural interventions: sociotechnical changes, job redesign and job enlargement, and job enrichment. The aim of sociotechnical interventions is to change the fit between the technological configurations, that is, task design and task assignments, and the social structure of work units. Most of the research done in this area has been in industrial systems—coal mines, cotton weaving mills, and so on. But, if we were to research a real situation like the mental hospital example above, especially on how the new organization of the ward teams will change the roles of both the professional staff and the paraprofessionals (ward aides, mental health technicians) and their interrelationships, we would have a nonindustrial example. If we concentrated on the human aspects of the intervention, on how the power relationships, the patterns of communication, the rearrangement of the physical environment, the interpersonal relationships, and so on, change during the period of transition and later, then we would have a report on a sociotechnical intervention of some importance.

By and large, however, there is little attention given to this critically important issue of the interrelationship between the technology of work and the role relationships among workers, especially in the nonindustrial world. There, rather than seeing reorganization as a means for arranging people and work into a more integrated structure, it is used for a variety of other purposes—to establish the authority of a new manager, to cover up conflict, to deal with external or internal criticism of the organization, and so on. Saper (1975) in a classic article, "Confessions of a former state hospital superintendent," tells the apocryphal story of being told, upon taking over from his predecessor, that there were three envelopes in his office safe. He was instructed to open these, each in turn, when he was in serious administrative trouble. Two months later, faced by the first crisis, he opened the envelope and a note was found,

"Blame me!" Six months later, in great despair, he opened the second note, "Reorganize!!" A year later, the third envelope was opened. It's message was "Prepare three envelopes!!!"

Unfortunately, the second message gets heard with even greater frequency that this story would indicate. Because the goals of non-industrial organizations are not completely clear, the structure needed to achieve these goals is even less clear. This double lack of clarity leads to frequent reorganizations, almost invariably with little impact on the overall functioning of the agency. Indeed, there are many organizations in which reorganizations occur so frequently that there is never an opportunity to test out whether or not the current reorganization would have any effect upon the functioning of the agency.

What tends to be ignored in these reorganizations, that are proposed on rational grounds, are the issues that make up the human experience—conflicts, misunderstandings, competencies or lack of them, and interpersonal and intergroup rivalries.

In one community drug abuse agency that was in great difficulty, a traditional consulting firm operating from an operations research approach was sent in as a resource by the federal agency monitoring the program. The Board of Directors, consisting of 75 well-intentioned, diverse community leaders, was unclear about the purpose of the organization and the board's role in it. The executive director, an incompetent person, spent most of his energy attempting to demonstrate simultaneously that he "ran the whole show" and that any errors of omission or commission on the part of the agency were the fault of incompetent others whom he was in the process of discharging. The staff was demoralized, confused about roles, and searching for leadership. The clients, addicts and former addicts, were quite unhappy about the limited and ineffectual services that they had been receiving. Two senior consultants from this traditional consulting organization spent two days interviewing the staff, primarily the executive director. They interviewed the executive committee of the board only at its insistence. About one

WORLD WIDE SYSTEMS

3636 NW 36 Street
Washington, D.C. 20036

Telephone (202) 336-3636

Washington   New York
Buffalo   Hong Kong

February 6, 1975

Mr. Fred Blank
Executive Director
Washington County Drug Abuse Council
East Oak Street
Anytown, Ohio

Dear Mr. Blank:

We would like to take this opportunity to thank you, your staff, and the Board of Directors for your cooperation on our recent information-gathering visit. We found all individuals receptive to our purpose and eager to assist us in understanding your programs and activities.

Currently, we are digesting and assimilating the detail that we captured. Recommendations are beginning to crystallize. As indicated by our work plan, we are working in two prime areas. First, we will provide recommendations as well as supporting rationale for the reorganization of the Council. This will include an action strategy to implement structural changes in the organization (including the Board), changes in certain functions, and training required for staff and Board members under the new organization. Second, we are designing the framework for an administrative policies and procedures manual for which the Council staff must identify and develop the actual procedures to be used. The World Wide Systems, Inc. (WWS), team will draft certain key parts of the manual to facilitate maintenance and further development by the staff.

These documents will be provided to the federal authorities for review and then forwarded to you approximately two weeks before our next site visit tentatively scheduled for the week of April 5. We will review them with you and other key Council, Board, and staff personnel to identify areas that must be revised and to clarify any problems.

Mr. Fred Blank
February 6, 1975
Page Two

Between now and March 15, we request that the Executive Committee, the Policy Committee, and the Executive Director work together to re-develop the Council's overall objectives, as stated in Article II of the By-Laws. This will be useful to Council and WWS since these objectives constitute the statements of the overall purpose of the organization. Basic functions for the organization are derived from such statements of purpose. Thus, a clear statement of the overall purpose of the Council is essential for the effective development of the reorganization.

To assist you in the process of redeveloping the Council's objectives, WWS has prepared and attached to this letter a Working Statement of Purpose. This guide is intended to lead the Council's officials in a positive direction in further clarifying objectives and goals of the organization. In addition to the Working Statement of Purpose and Article II of the By-Laws, a thorough review of the Articles of Incorporation would be prudent at this time. This is recommended, since it appears that no significant review of the purpose of the organization has taken place in seven years, excepting the addition of the "prevention objective."

We have not yet received the revised Board policies drafted recently by the Policy Committee. We are eager to review this document and provide assistance in finalizing Board policies.

If we can be of assistance in clarifying further any aspect of this request of the Council, please do not hesitate to contact us.

Yours sincerely,

WORLD WIDE SYSTEMS

Homer Hardy
Vice-President

Attachment

Fig. 7.1   An example of a reorganizational proposal that is not a sociotechnical intervention. Source: Actual letter received by a drug abuse agency with only the identifying data changed.

month after their visit, the letter presented in Fig. 7.1 was received by the executive director.

During the site visit during the week of April 5, the details of the letter were essentially restated and the council was left with the task of implementing a reorganization of itself based upon the rationally derived guidelines of a policies and procedures manual. While the consultants did recognize that one of the central issues confronting the organization was the lack of clarity of goals and purposes, their recommendation for a solution—the development of a statement of purpose within six weeks—suggests that such a statement within a time limit would promote direct behavioral consequences. The clear fact that there was strong and long-standing disagreement among both staff and board about the organization's purpose—for instance, the relative emphasis to be placed on treatment or prevention—was essentially overlooked, as were the failures of the executive director over his two-year tenure. When these issues were brought to the attention to the consultation team, they were airily dismissed with the statement, "We never get involved in intraorganizational political issues." Our reasons for concluding that this intervention did not meet the criteria of a sociotechnical one is that the underlying social structure on which the organization was based was unexplored and that the human processes that are necessary to reach agreement on organizational goals were completely neglected.

One useful procedure for helping organizations develop greater goal clarity is the Nominal Group Procedure, developed by André Delbecq (Delbecq and van de Ven, 1971). In this process, any group of six to eight participants, regardless of role, works individually to define and identify the critical problems facing the organization. The group is "nominal" as the individuals work in the presence of others but do not interact verbally. The focus of the group's activity is on "problem-centering," not on "problem-solution." If there are more than six to eight persons to be involved, they can work in any number of small groups with each group seated around a table.

Each participant is given a stack of index cards and asked to write one organizational problem on each card and one personal feeling on the back of that card. At the end of 30 minutes, the organizational problems are read aloud in a round-robin fashion and posted on a large sheet of newsprint. If several participants have identified the same organizational problem, a tally of these is posted next to the listed item. The same procedure is then followed for the personal feelings. After some general discussion about the nature of the items, the group is asked to vote on which of the many problems listed would be considered the five most important and which personal feelings are the most important. The final products of all the nominal groups participating in such an exercise can then be combined to produce an overall problem and feeling census. Not only can this process be used to identify problems but it can also be used to identify activities to which the organization should be devoting its energies. Its use is to help individuals openly state both how they feel and what they perceive about the organization in which they work.

Our criticisms of the attempt to reform the drug abuse agency through a restructuring should not suggest that such interventions may not have impact on the organization, even a salutory effect. In the case of the psychology department reported in Chapter 6, the structural arrangement of three graduate programs gave the curriculum power to the three graduate program committees. The creation of two new superordinate committees—one on graduate studies and one on undergraduate studies with the three graduate programs working through the former—had considerable impact on the policymaking processes of this department. While the need and potential utility of this structure was developed at a day-long retreat in which the Nominal Groups Procedure was used, there was a long period of time before the new organization actually began to function smoothly. Thus, despite the attention paid to the human processes involved in creating some structural change in an organization and despite the fact that the changes were internally mandated, there was a long period before the changes, and the implicit goals they represented, were fully accepted by the members of the organization.

The remaining two technostructural interventions—job design and job enlargement, and job enrichment—have had almost no attention in the nonindustrial sector. While sociotechnical interventions focus on the whole system, more or less, job design or job enlargement tend to focus upon sets of interrelated functions, and job enrichment typically involves a single job. Both job design and job enrichment attempt to increase job satisfaction and job performance by creating jobs in which there is greater variety, autonomy, discretion, personal identification with product, and responsibility for work. Typically, job design or enlargement involves combining several jobs into one job that several workers can do. Thus workers have the opportunity to vary their activities during any given time period and the entire team is responsible for that phase of the process rather than having each separate phase assigned to a particular worker. In terms of our more theoretical discussion in Chapter 4, many functions which had been differentiated and assigned to individuals were recombined and assigned to teams.

The most widely known example of this approach is the Volvo Motor Car Corporation of Sweden where teams are given whole subunits to assemble. This approach also has a number of American applications, all in the private sector. While there is now a good bit of evidence to support the contention that such job redesign does lead to both increased satisfaction and productivity (see Friedlander and Brown, 1974, pp. 322–323, for a summary of this literature), none of these studies involve white collar or clerical workers. The values explicit in this approach run contrary to the bureaucratic notion that given tasks must be the sole responsibility of particular workers and that the failure to assign either task or responsibility leads to organizational breakdown. Also the large number of professional and subprofessional workers who continue to work in human services suggests that boredom and a lack of a

sense of task accomplishment may be irrelevant issues in these systems. Until there is some research on these issues in the nonindustrial sector, however, the usefulness of developing job design and
job enrichment intervention strategies in this sector will not be
known.

Process Interventions

Process interventions are ones that are concerned with those human
processes like communication, problem solving and decision making, and conflict management, by which organizational goals are
met or fail to be met. Process interventions are the change strategies
utilized by the process consultation approach outlined in Chapter 3.
Friedlander and Brown (1974) identify three kinds of process interventions which have been the target of some research: survey feedback, group development or team building, and intergroup development or system building. To this list, we would add one-to-one
coaching or consulting which, despite the fact that it has not been
adequately researched, is an important process intervention.

Since earlier in this chapter we have provided a case of coaching
and counseling, perhaps only a little more needs to be said in its
behalf. If the diagnosis clearly points out that leadership is an issue,
then the leader will certainly question what behavioral changes will
achieve the desired result. Counseling and coaching can even be
critical when there are structural issues involved as well as leadership ones, as the leadership may need support and planning help in
figuring out how the structural matters can be managed.

In approaching his or her task, the consultant must be certain
that the client who is the target of coaching and counseling has
emotionally accepted the fact that personal changes are necessary
and that what the consultant is proposing is a collaborative relationship in which the client can propose new behaviors, these new
behaviors will be evaluated in terms of possible consequences, then

will be tried out and the actual consequences compared with those predicted. The same techniques and criteria which skilled counselors and psychotherapists use to assess counseling readiness in a clinical situation are equally useful here. Indeed, such counseling involves a clinical relationship and is based upon the same theoretical assumptions as any other clinical relationship, except that it is conducted in the client's office rather than the counselor's.

There is one rather tricky issue that needs to be kept in mind. As we work with a member of the organizational team in such a one-to-one relationship, the focus must be on how the client handles organizational problems. Since it is usually difficult to separate out family and other personal matters from organizational issues, the consultant needs to remember that this is not a general purpose counseling relationship but one focused on organizational improvement. For instance, if the client discusses how his wife relates to his job and the problems that ensue, this would appear to be a legitimate topic to pursue, as working this issue through will probably benefit the organization. But if the client moves on to more general family issues, like child rearing and the like, then the organizational payoff is not so clear. While it can be argued that any improvement in the client's life is probably going to have some positive implications for his or her work, the consultant role as a coach and counselor is not to provide general therapeutic help. Our recommendation is that, when it becomes apparent that there is a need for longer-term or more extensive counseling than would seem appropriate under the terms of the consultant's contract with the client, it is time to refer the client elsewhere. Consultants with strong clinical backgrounds may find this difficult to do and, in any event, *when* to refer is usually a difficult decision to make.

Survey Feedback

To return to the kinds of process interventions that have been researched, survey feedback is the process by which data that have been systematically collected from organizational members are fed back in some organized and summarized form to those portions of the organization which provided them. The two primary forms of data that are fed back are from interviews and questionnaires. Many writers in this area tend to restrict the term survey feedback to questionnaire data alone, but there is no compelling reason for such a restriction. For example, if the consultant, using Weisbord's Six-Box Model outlined in Chapter 6, interviews all the senior managers in a welfare agency and finds no agreement on the purpose of the agency, such data, when fed back, should be as useful as any data from a questionnaire. The basic assumption underlying the use of survey feedback as a process intervention is that whatever discrepancies are found and reported between the organization's ideal and its actual practices or performance will serve as an impetus for reform. Thus, if most of the staff of some help-providing agency see the agency as doing harm rather than providing help, this ought to be an alarming datum to all concerned.

As we have noted repeatedly throughout the course of this book, the process consultation model which we are following requires the establishment of a strong norm of collaboration between the consultant and the client. The consultant may play the primary role in designing the questionnaires or interviews, collecting the actual data, analyzing and organizing the data for presentation, actually presenting the data, planning for follow-up, and processing the data presentation session. Nevertheless, throughout this process there must be active collaboration and involvement by significant portions of the client system, otherwise the data may well be distrusted. Since the consultant is regarded as an expert in the technology of questionnaire and interview construction, it is easy for many consultants to slip from the collaborative to the expert role at this point—thus caution is needed here.

Early and continual participation is necessary, and the client may either help draft items or may pass on the appropriate items drafted by the consultant. Further, all of the affected subunits and significant individuals of the organization to be surveyed need to be involved, especially those playing leadership and linkage roles. We have frequently found it useful to brief key managers about the nature of certain aspects of the feedback prior to the general meeting in which the data are to be presented. Thus, if an agency supervisor is to be told that there are serious reservations about the management style in his or her unit, a prior discussion of these findings ordinarily will reduce his or her defensiveness and inspire him or her to review the behavior in question and open up alternatives before the feedback session with the unit is scheduled. It must be underscored that we are not suggesting that any punches be pulled or that data be concealed, but that some prior work may be an effective way of opening rather than closing channels of communication.

It would seem apparent that survey feedback is a powerful tool to identify attitudinal concerns in an organization. In fact, the high impact of survey feedback is the most obvious reason for including it as an intervention rather than a diagnostic procedure. The very collection of these data suggests to the organization's members that their ideas are important, and the open feedback further confirms this. Thus it is critical that all persons who help produce the data participate in the feedback session. However, any extensive organizational change requires more than just survey feedback. Plans of action need to be developed and, again, the role of the consultant in such plans needs to be renegotiated. Rather than being a final intervention, survey feedback interventions tend to serve as a bridge between the diagnostic and following intervention activities. We will return to this point in Chapter 8.

Group Development on Team Building

Team building, or group development, interventions are "probably the most important single group of (OD) interventions" (French and Bell, 1973, p. 112). The particular issues that are dealt with in any given team-building sessions will, of course, depend upon the diagnosis involved. While the consultant is typically the expert on the design and conduct of such sessions, the overall plan to be used needs to be shared and agreed upon with the client.

Such sessions are typically conducted away from the usual work site in an informal atmosphere, both to avoid the distractions of work demands and to facilitate some risk taking that might not occur under ordinary circumstances. There are a variety of exercises or "games" that are often used during such workshops. Such exercises, together with their theoretical rationale, have been developed to help resolve a number of typical problems such as increasing the level of openness and trust within a work unit, increasing the openness of the unit to face its own problems rather than "sweep them under the rug," comparing the formal and informal structures of the organization, comparing one's personal ideology with that of the organization, and generally producing greater participation of all members in the work and management of the organization. The interested reader will find the *Annual Handbook for Group Facilitators*, published since 1972, by the University Associates (7596 Eads Avenue, La Jolla, California) a veritable treasure of such exercises. While some circumstances might lead to rather unstructured T-group or sensitivity training with the unit, these exercises do tend to provide a clearer focus for the group's activity, at least at the beginning of the team-building session.

Such sessions can be regarded as temporary systems (Miles, 1964) which may begin to induce lasting changes in the permanent system of the organization. Such a temporary system, because of its clearly limited time and its psychological isolation from both the organization's usual roles and work demands, can give the participants freedom to express themselves more honestly and less defensively. Following such openness, alternatives can be developed for making changes on both the individual and group levels. The norm of the workshop, that of "playing a game," can free the participants from many of the personal and organizational constraints that ordinarily limit openness. The most serious problem involved in such sessions is how to link the understanding and resolve that results back to the job site. This, of course, is a familiar problem to any counselor or psychotherapist.

The following example, while drawn from an industrial organization, could just as well have involved a human service system and does represent many of the principles of team-building workshops. Harold, a self-critical and rather "straight" engineer, had been appointed plant manager at the newly constructed unit of a high-technology manufacturing organization. He was very aware that the rest of his management team was troubled by his appointment and that there was little cohesion among the members. Interviews with this staff revealed that the engineering manager, Fred, who had served as interim plant manager until Harold's arrival, was badly disappointed that he had not been appointed permanent plant manager. Fred had many loyal followers among the management group who felt that he had deserved the post. Harold had been plant manager at a smaller plant owned by the same organization. During this earlier period, he had been less than completely successful, at least in his own eyes. He was seen, however, by corporate management as one of the "rising stars" of the organization and was given the new post as a promotion, although it was not one that he had requested.

Upon taking over, Harold played a "waiting game," often deferring decisions to Fred who had more information. At the time the consultation began, it was clear that Harold had never really exercised his new leadership role and his staff was confused about the role he was to take. Since he was self-critical, he tended to dwell on the negative rather than the positive portions of his previous assignment when he discussed his transfer with his staff, and this confused them even further.

During the team-building session, members of the staff, including Harold, were asked to construct individual lists of the characteristics of a "successful manager" and then combine their lists into a single one. During this exercise, Harold again failed to take a leadership role, a fact which became the focus of the group's attention during the processing period following the conclusion of the task. The consultant facilitated the group's discussion of the circumstances of Harold's arrival, his failure to take charge, the negative expectations of him, the existent loyalty to Fred, and a number of other issues. By the end of a long, nine-hour session, Harold was able to see some changes that were necessary in his behavior, and the group heard, for the first time, his intention to "be" the plant manager, and Fred's willingness to serve in his appropriate role as engineering manager. Over time, most of this came to pass, although Harold's relationship with Fred continued to be less than satisfactory.

In this example we can see the focus on the diagnosis in the exercise used in the initial portion of the team-building session, and how the "temporary system" enabled the group to deal with issues that otherwise would have remained covert and would have continued to affect the quality of the work produced. Friedlander and Brown (1974, p. 329), in summarizing the few research studies of team building within organizations, conclude that there is "convergent evidence that group development (team building) activities affect participant attitudes and sometimes their behavior as well." Clearly, more research is needed but it is also clear that such team building is the heart of most OD work at this time.

Intergroup Development or System Building

Intergroup development, or system building, is the last of the process interventions covered by Friedlander and Brown. They note that problems at the interface between units or groups within organizations are endemic in modern society and because such problems interfere with the necessary integration of such units, they are of considerable importance to organizational consultants. While a number of strategies have been suggested for dealing with such problems (e.g., Walton, 1969; Lorsch and Lawrence, 1972), the usual approach to such situations is not very different from that used in unit team building, although the focus is on the difficulties between subunits rather than on those between individuals. System-building workshops focusing on information sharing, confrontation of differences, and working through such differences in the pursuit of understanding and harmony are the typical strategies involved.

A community job-retraining center requested consultation help because it was not able to service effectively the clients it was receiving (Goodstein, 1972). An organizational diagnosis revealed that there were two bureaucracies involved in the running of the center—the state division of vocational rehabilitation and the municipal board of education—and that there was considerable distrust and misunderstanding between the members of these two organizations, although they were supposed to be working as a single team in the servicing of clients.

After the diagnosis was firmly established, and with the consent of representatives of both organizations, a system-building workshop was held. The major device used was a stereotyping exercise, one which Friedlander and Brown (1974, p. 330) term the "prototype design" for such interventions. The members of the two bureaucracies were asked to meet separately and to develop a list of seven adjectives that best described its own group and that best described the other group. A consultant sat in with each group to "keep them honest" and to act as a process observer. The combined group then reassembled and the data from the two groups were posted. As one would anticipate, each of the two groups tended to be self-praising while being rather derogatory of the other. "We" are always dedicated, sincere, and professional, while "you" are bureaucratic, unrealistic, and bumbling. New groups were developed with a mixture of members from the two subunits and they were instructed to discuss these discrepant perceptions, again with a consultant sitting in as a process observer. This interaction did much to clarify how these differing perceptions had interfered with the functioning of the organization as a whole. Of course, such a workshop is only a first step in resolving such subunit discord, but it can serve as the initiation of a continuing process.

While there is little research evidence on the effectiveness of such system-building interventions, they do seem to follow the model of team development and, hopefully, the evidence will be both forthcoming and supportive. What can be observed in both the case of team and system building, however, is the strong reliance on process consultation and the diagnostic phase upon which the interventions are built.

Later Stages
in Consultation

Criteria to Judge
Change

We began this volume by noting that organizations experience problems or desire change as do individuals and families. These problems lead organizations to seek professional help—consultation—just as individuals seek professional help—counseling or psychotherapy. Once there is a reduction in the severity of the problems, or merely an amelioration of the surface symptoms, there is a strong tendency on the part of individuals, families, and organizations to withdraw from their professionally helpful relationships, often prematurely from the professional's point of view.

While we clearly recognize that professional helpers or consultants have a vested interest, often financial, in maintaining relationships with their clients, it can also be noted that clients are often too willing to accept superficial improvements or symptom reduction as successful cures or resolutions of the underlying problems. Rather than viewing such symptom reduction as the beginning of a change process that needs to be stabilized, the client all too often attempts to terminate the counseling relationship with profuse thanks for a job well done. For example, the job-retraining agency described in Chapter 7 terminated the relationship with the consultant after the initial workshop with the members of the organization seeing the glow of good feelings that emerged from the workshop as a sign that the organization's problems had been resolved. It is true that continued consultation may have altered the later governmental decision not to refund the agency for a second year. Nevertheless, the agency's failure to establish a clearly articulated set of goals and a functional plan for achieving these goals could have hardly impressed the funding organizations.

On the other hand, clients can become too dependent upon a consultant. Rather than facilitating the communication processes of the organization, the consultant can become the sole channel of communication. Rather than helping the client learn more about effective decision-making procedures, the consultant may become the decision maker. In one organization, the norm developed that important decisions were made only at those weekly staff meetings which the consultant attended, usually one a month. The other three meetings were regarded as a waste of time for the agency members who attended because no significant decisions could be made without the consultant's presence and approval.

Since while both of these extremes obviously need to be avoided, what, then, are the limits of a successful consultation; in other words, when can a consultant beneficially terminate a relationship with a client? The consensual diagnosis arrived at by the client and consultant, and the consultation contract which should flow from that diagnosis, should provide a partial answer. When the group has been modified so that there has been institutionalization of the changes necessary to avoid recurrences of the problems identified in the diagnosis, then the intervention may be regarded as a success and the consultant should be able to terminate the intensive relationship with the client. But such institutionalized change takes commitment, time, and energy on the part of both the client and the consultant.

What do we mean by the institutionalization of change? We mean that the norms and values of the organization have been modified in some more-or-less permanent way so that the diagnosed problems are unlikely to interfere with organizational effectiveness or the satisfactions of the members of the groups. Thus, conflicts will be handled directly rather than being avoided, organizational goals will have been clarified and there will be a reasonable commitment to these goals by the majority of the organization's members, there will be confidence that the leadership is ready to provide a strong and continual guidance, and the members of the group will have acquired adequate skills to implement the new norms and values in their daily work. Necessary changes may mean that members of the organization need to develop better communication skills so that they can "check out" their perceptions of what they "see" is happening before they react; or that the procedures for developing consensual agreement about a plan of action need to be acquired by a more significant portion of the membership; or that people may have to learn how to confront each other about differences without forcing one or the other to abandon a position. The development of these skills and the integration of the new norms and values take time but it is the function of the consultant to arrange learning opportunities for members to gain the required new skills.

Much of this training is done in experiential workshops which the consultant or others conduct with small groups. These human-relations skills workshops, which form an integral part of many interventions, have caused some consultants to be called "trainers," especially those whose primary skills are in the conduct of such workshops. It is also permissible for organization members to attend training workshops in human-relations skills (sensitivity training), conflict management, performance appraisal, and communications skills outside of the organization. However it may be acquired, the development of such skills by a significant portion of the members is an important element of most long-term interventions.

Changing the norms and values of organizations so that there will be more interpersonal openness is quite difficult to accomplish. The majority of organizations have little experience with such openness and are quite fearful about making efforts to attain it. Argyris (1969) has reported extensive data bearing on this general point.

He studied 163 group meetings of 10 different organizations involving 400 people. Each of these meetings was a work session devoted to such important issues as long-range planning, investment policy, and personnel problems. Each meeting was tape recorded with the permission of the participants so that the actual interchanges could be analyzed later. The 163 sessions yielded 45,803 scorable behavioral units.

Argyris' data suggest that there are two typical patterns which can occur in such work sessions. Pattern A involves the sharing of a person's own ideas, interest in the world of ideas, and a generalized commitment to ideas. Rarely observed is the expression of a person's feelings, interest in the feelings of others, or experimenting with feelings. Questions of trust or mistrust, concern with the individuality of group members, or the satisfaction of the group with the quality of the meeting are rarely considered. In Pattern A people rarely say what they think, especially if what they think is threatening to anyone else. Rather they prefer to be "diplomatic," "careful," and "not make waves." Problem solving under these circumstances is difficult as the important issues are never addressed and important information is covered up.

Pattern B is characterized by the open expression of feelings, by open risk taking in both ideas and feelings, by helping others to express both ideas and feelings, and by the norm of individuality and trust being more pronounced than the norms of conformity and antagonism.

Pattern A behavior was evidenced in approximately 90 percent of the behavioral units in the groups studied, Pattern B behavior in only 10 percent of the scorable units. Even more striking, however, is Argyris' meeting-by-meeting analysis of these data. In 56 percent of the meetings no feelings were ever discussed. In another 24 percent, less than 1 percent of the behaviors involved feelings. In one session in which there were 23 percent feeling behaviors and another in which there were 35 percent, members experienced a high degree of personal stress. Following one of these highly affective meetings Argyris reports that the president apologized to him for the "childish immaturity" of the participants and promised not to allow this to happen again. It did not!

While we are not suggesting that staff or other task meetings should become psychological "blood baths," it should be clear that there are feelings involved in most meetings and that our failure to process these data is a major factor in the high degree of dissatisfaction that most people report about such activities. Further, the failure to encourage risk taking, both with ideas and feelings, leads to a poorer-quality decision-making process than would otherwise be true.

The purpose of citing Argyris' data at this point, however, is to highlight the difficulties inherent in changing organizational norms. Without belaboring the importance of Pattern B behaviors, the problem is how to produce and stabilize an increase in them. The very low frequency of these behaviors in most organizations, the low skill of most members in these behaviors, the lack of certainty that such behaviors will improve organizational life, and the generalized resistance to change all combine to make this change difficult to achieve.

While improving the quality of staff meetings sounds like an important and reasonable goal for consultation, if this is assumed to mean increasing Pattern B behaviors—increased openness and greater individual honesty—then the consultant and client are committed to many hours of intensive work together over a long period of time. The critical test of such a change is the degree to which such behaviors begin to occur on a regular basis when the consultant is not present. Then, and only then, can the consultant and client begin to believe that the changes are institutionalized. With the institutionalization of change—in this case when open staff meetings are the norm—the activity level of the consultant can be reduced without the fear that previous efforts will be of little lasting impact.

We have previously indicated that the consultant, in moving into a relationship with a client, is attempting to change or modify some ongoing patterns of behavior, to break an unfavorable cycle of behavior. It is a truism that these pre-existing patterns have advantages for the client for without these positive consequences the behaviors would not have become institutionalized in the first place. Indeed, all clients (individual or organizational) operate in such a fashion as to maximize the positive consequences of their behavior in their present situation. While there are always costs as a consequence of any behavior, the existing pattern of behaviors can be seen as the best possible cost-benefit compromise that the client apparently can arrange.

As Platt (1973) has noted, however, the long-term costs often outweigh the short-term benefits, a situation he labels as a "social trap." One of the catalytic functions which a consultant often serves is the highlighting of long-term negative consequences that the client can easily "overlook." For example, in working with a client system that was both growing rapidly and committed to a pattern of nearly exclusive internal promotions, the consultant pointed out that continued future growth at the same rate would not be possible without external recruitment. It can be noted that clients are hardly ever willing either to accept the interpretation that they are in a "social trap" or to be grateful to those who point out the difficulty.

The observation that the client is receiving some positive yield from certain behaviors means that there is bound to be some resistance to giving up this yield (despite the cost) for some unknown consequence. Lewin (1947) in his now-classic analysis of the process of planned change identified the first step of the process as "unfreezing." By unfreezing he meant identifying the need to give up habitual or stereotyped behaviors that are well integrated into one's behavior. All of the consultant's interventions (discussed in the previous chapter) that permit the client system to understand its present level of functioning, and the negative consequences of this functioning, can be seen as unfreezing procedures. Also "unfreezing" would be the encouragement of the client to consider behavioral alternatives or new norms.

Lewin's second step in planned change is "moving to a new level," where the new behaviors are attempted and the client system develops some skills in these behaviors. At this point the consultant needs to assist the client not to become discouraged. Since any new set of behaviors is initially awkward and uncomfortable, the tendency to give them up and return to an older and more comfortable mode of operation is a rather typical and understandable response. As we suggested earlier, the consultant's level of activity during this phase is intensive as he or she organizes and manages team-building workshops, skills-development programs, coaching, and other strategies to integrate the new behaviors.

The final stage of Lewin's approach to planned change is "freezing" the group's behavior at the new level. By freezing (or perhaps "refreezing" might be better) Lewin means the stabilization and generalization of change. In other words, the new behaviors have become part of the client's norm and are self-sustaining. In the terms of our earlier discussion, the changes which the client and consultant have collaboratively agreed upon have been institutionalized.

Terminating a Consulting Relationship

Throughout the earlier section of this chapter we have emphasized both the difficulties of creating planned change in organizations and the criteria by which we would like to have these change efforts judged. When these difficulties are overcome and results meet the objectives, the client and consultant then need to consider termination of their relationship.

In preparation, the consultant needs to begin suggesting some reduction in the intensity of the relationship when there are some signs that the agreed-upon changes are becoming stabilized. For example, where the consultant may have been serving as a process observer at weekly staff meetings, the frequency may be initially reduced to once a month, then to once a quarter, and finally, to availability "on call." He or she wants to remain available to help with newly emerging problems. The consultant's gradual withdrawal simultaneously provides a test of the degree of institutionalization of the changes and the degree of dependence of the client. As we know, by now the impetus for continuing the new behaviors should be internal. If this is not the case and the changes in norms and values erode in a brief time, the consultation has failed.

Throughout the consultation process, and especially in the terminal phase, internal resources in the client system need to be identified—people who have both the commitment and the skills to maintain and extend the changes that have been initiated. It is hoped that these resources are people with sufficient status and power to influence the course of events in the organization's future. Unfortunately, however, many times the responsibility for both linkage with the consultant and sustaining the changes is given to the personnel or training unit, subunits which ordinarily have low "clout" with the rest of the organization. It would be preferable to have a task force of senior managers for then the maintenance and extension of the planned change becomes a line management responsibility (Foltz, Harvey, and McLaughlin, 1974).

One may question if consultation is ever truly terminated. Sigmund Freud (1950), commenting on the problems of terminating individual psychotherapy in his article, "Psychoanalysis: Terminable or interminable," suggests that the individual therapist cannot inoculate the client or patient against new problems, but can only help solve current problems. Therapists, therefore, need to be available to and have a cordial relationship with their patients or clients in order to serve as a helpful resource when new problems emerge. It should be understood that difficulties experienced with new problems are not a failure of the earlier therapy.

If this is true of individuals, it is even more true of organizations. There is a changing membership, with members leaving or taking on new roles or being replaced by others with different values and expectations. This is coupled with changes in goals, all of which creates more instability in organizations than is typically found with individuals. The wise and experienced consultant, like the veteran therapist, recognizes that there is a good possibility that circumstances will arise in the future that will again lead the organization to require intervention.

Roles Consultants Play

Another way of describing the consultation process is through an examination of the several roles that consultants play. Steele (1975) has suggested that there are least nine such roles, any of which can occur in the process of consultation with a single client. Also, the role(s) that the consultant plays can change through the course of a consultation.

An examination of these roles at the juncture can provide both a review and an overview of the consultation process. Obviously these roles are not mutually exclusive and the wise consultant rather deliberately chooses the role he or she wishes to play at any given moment. The choice would depend upon the diagnosis of the client system and the nature of the planned intervention.

The first of the roles mentioned by Steele is that of *teacher*. The consultant as teacher provides the client with new information and insights into the organizational world, especially the interpersonal world. The teacher may range from teaching about matrix organizations to introducing Transactional Analysis, but he or she always is offering some new ways in which the client may understand the issues that need to be faced. In playing this role, the consultant is using a theory-and-principles type of intervention, according to the Consulcube (see Chapter 2).

The *student* role is the second of Steele's consultant roles. The consultant as a professional is always eager to extend his or her understanding of organizational life. Like most other professionals, organizational consultants are ready to accept difficult or challenging clients—clients from whom they will learn both about the organization and its problems and about the process of consultation. If they have never worked with an organization undergoing rapid growth or one involved in community action or a rural school district, then they are interested in them as clients. This is not to suggest that consultants view new clients as "guinea pigs" or experimental subjects, but their own commitment to their professional growth demands this kind of challenge.

The third of the roles consultants play is that of *barbarian*. The barbarian asks the unaskable, says the unsayable. The consultant as barbarian confronts the organization with the Emperor's nakedness. For instance, as part of his or her process observation of a client organization, a consultant brought the group up short by observing the norm of the "left-handed compliment." Rather than directly complimenting or thanking someone for a job well done, organizational members typically would note that "Joe didn't screw this one up" or "Mary made an exception this time and got the job completed by the deadline." The consultant was criticized initially for "not understanding" the intended humor. But, when he persisted in his "barbarian" ways, others present began to express their discomfort with this norm and indicate their longing for some more direct positive feedback. The consultant's role as a confronter of destructive or nonfunctional norms is perhaps the most valuable of all those in his or her repertoire.

Consultants also serve as *detectives*, attempting to uncover the underlying reasons for the client's problems. The development of an adequate diagnosis requires that the consultant be sensitive to subtle clues, that he or she collect evidence and order the findings to identify root causes. In order to fulfill this role, consultants need to understand patterns of individual behavior, sometimes called psychodynamics, as well as patterns of organizational behavior. As an example of the former, a consulting team encountered an organizational controller whose suspiciousness verged on paranoia. In his efforts to control inappropriate expenditures he so carefully scrutinized travel and other expense vouchers that many such vouchers remained unpaid over months, arousing considerable antagonism and causing lowered morale. Transferring voucher approval to another individual greatly improved the organizational climate.

As a sample of detective work on an organizational level, we can cite the case of a community mental health center whose staff meeting were poorly attended and whose staff members were rather passive. The staff meetings were supposed to plan treatment programs for the center's patients and to provide continuing review of the adopted programs. Consultation help was requested to make the meetings more functional. Careful inquiry over time made it apparent that a central issue underlying the problem was that the center's medical staff did not feel bound by decisions reached at the staff meetings. While the psychiatrists felt that medical responsibility required them to increase or decrease tranquilizers and other drugs as they thought necessary, the rest of the staff felt that patients were manipulating the medical staff in order to vitiate the agreed-upon plan. In any event the failure of the medical staff to adhere to the staff plan made the staff meetings appear to be a waste of time in the view of the nonmedical personnel who participated. None of this, however, had been openly discussed at a staff meeting and the agency director was completely unaware of it.

A fifth role that consultants can play is that of *timekeeper*. Organizations, like individuals, can have problems managing time, both in the short and long run. One organization, for example, always "ran out of time" at staff meetings before substantive issues were addressed. Thus planning and goal setting were never discussed. Another organization never set a target deadline for an activity such as establishing an affirmative action plan, or, when such deadlines *were* set, they were conveniently ignored. The consultant can play the role of timekeeper, gently or not so gently, reminding the organization of the overlooked deadline or of the failure to set a deadline. Just the fact of regularly scheduled visits can serve as a time signal to the organization that certain actions or behaviors are now necessary. While calling "time" may be seen as a special case of the consultant as barbarian, the role of time management is so central to organizational life that timekeeping should be seen as a separate and distinct role for the consultant.

The consultant also serves as a *talisman*, or symbol. As an outsider to the organization, and a person who often represents different values, the consultant is a visible symbol of change. His or her mere physical presence is often enough to produce considerable difference in the conduct of an organization. During one five-hour staff meeting a consultant literally said nothing. He was rather surprised when one of the participants after the meeting thanked him profusely "for all that he had done." When he pointed out that he had been silent through the course of the meeting, the participant after some thought indicated that his mere presence had been adequate to make this one of the organization's most productive planning sessions. It would appear that the consultant with known values and process skills who can intervene when necessary does serve a purpose in keeping the group honest.

But, of course, the consultant's symbolic role is usually not sufficient and he or she must also serve as an *advocate*. As we have tried to make clear, process consultation involves a firm value position. Our model of consultation includes a commitment to the integrity and dignity of individuals, the integration of individual and organizational goals, open communications, and authenticity of interpersonal relationships. The process consultant in all of his or her activities—diagnosis, intervention, or evaluation—is an advocate for these values. In processing the conflict-free norm of a staff meeting, in coaching a manager on how to provide more adequate performance appraisal, in designing a communication skills workshop, or in developing a feedback session or evaluation instrument, the consultant's commitment to and advocacy of these values is essential. Otherwise, the process merely becomes a superficial distraction from real concerns.

The role of *monitor* is yet another of the roles that consultants play. The client and consultant usually agree that there are certain behaviors that are central to the causes of the client's problem. The consultant as monitor observes the client system in action and, as objectively as possible, points out these behaviors when it is clear they are becoming problematic and have been unnoticed by the client system. For example, in providing the client system with feedback about the quality of staff decisions, the consultant points out that task forces are created to "look into" certain issues, but no time frame for reporting back is ever set and these task forces are never asked for reports. As a consequence, most of the task forces take their charge rather casually instead of seriously tackling their assignments. When this was pointed out to the agency staff, there was immediate and uniform agreement that this was a real problem and required corrective action. The consultant agreed to help monitor this behavior and point it out whenever it appeared to be overlooked by the agency staff. Consultants thus monitor the client system according to their own appraisal of the behavior and using their own notions of effective task performance.

The last of Steele's consultant's role is that of *sacrificial lamb,* or the ritual pig. Consultants are an expendable commodity and are often used by organizations to surface issues that are "too hot to handle" by insiders or to advocate unpopular or risky approaches to problems. Insiders have their jobs to protect and consultants have only a contract to lose. It is easy to move from consultant as barbarian to consultant as sacrificial lamb. The Emperor is not always delighted to be identified in his nakedness.

We have several times made reference to our consultation with a big city health department (Goodstein and Boyer, 1972). Despite our success in this case—gaining the resignation of the controversial health commissioner, reconstituting the Board of Health, and initiating the reorganization of the department—we were never again asked to be consultants. Even with our knowledge of the department and its workings, when new problems arose, other consultants were invited instead. The consultants, as well as the old board members and the commissioner, were sacrificed to the continued life of the organization.

Consultants as Marginal Employees

Regardless of the role(s) that the consultant plays, it is almost always a lonely role. Consultants, by nature of their function, are marginal people to the organizations with which they work. Indeed, it can be argued that their very marginality, their externality, is essential to their objectivity and, hence, their effectiveness. Their marginal status facilitates their playing their roles of barbarian, detective, timekeeper, talisman, advocate, and sacrificial lamb. Organizational members who have essential positions cannot ever play these roles without losing their centrality (and perhaps even their jobs), thus these roles are always left to the external consultant.

The roles, however, are difficult and uncomfortable ones for people to play. To always be an outsider, at least partially, to never feel part of an ongoing, functional organization requires some special attributes or, at least, unusual kinds of people. Little is known about the kinds of people who are attracted to the role of external consultant and even less is known about the personal qualities that bring success in this role. Browne, Cotton, and Golembiewski (1977) have clearly shown that external consultants, as compared to internal consultants, have a significantly more marginal orientation, as measured by the Ziller (1973) Self-Other Orientation Task. The internal consultants were, in turn, more marginal than the sample of salespersons and first-line supervisors used as a comparison group. Browne, Cotton, and Golembiewski emphasize the positive characteristics of marginality—neutrality, openmindedness, and adaptability in problem solving. They further point out that marginal people thrive on conflict, ambiguity, and stress. These qualities enable the external consultant to develop and maintain a perspective and detachment from the client's problem that can be uniquely useful to the client. We clearly need more data on the characteristics that should be developed in those being trained as consultants.

In a similar manner, Argyris (1970) notes that consultants live in two different worlds: the world of the client and the professional world of the consultant. Neither of these two worlds, however, can become the home base for the successful consultant. Consultants who move too far into the world of the client tend to accept the norms, values, and expectations of the client and, as a result, lose their precious objectivity. On the other hand, if they move too far into their own professional world, they can be seen as too professional, too detached and remote from the problems of the client system. This overprofessionalism interferes with the communication of trust, respect, and understanding necessary for a successful client-consultant relationship. The dilemma creates a continual conflict for many consultants as they try to balance the appeals of the two worlds.

What is apparent, however, is that consultants most frequently work alone and often far from their home bases. While most consultants would prefer to work in pairs, or in larger groups, the costs to the client system almost always prevents this from happening. The loneliness of the long-distance consultant is apparent to anyone who cares to inquire. Because the solo consultant far from home with only marginal linkages to the client organization is lonely, one needs to be concerned about how this loneliness affects the objectivity and clarity of his or her perceptions.

In an effort both to maintain their objectivity and to secure some personal support for their professional work, many consultants develop a relationship with a *shadow consultant* (Schroeder, 1974). Such a relationship provides a consultant to the consultant, much in the fashion of Caplan's (1970) case consultation. The relationship can be either formal or informal and can be either client- or consultee-centered, depending on whether the problem which is presented to the shadow consultant focuses on the issues presented by the client or issues in the consultant's own professional behavior (see Chapter 2). The shadow consultant, in either case, provides a noninvolved, even more objective, sounding board to review the consultants' role, and the diagnosis and intervention proposed.

Schroeder, in discussing the role of the shadow consultant, emphasizes the need for reciprocal trust between the two consultants and the need for the shadow consultant to avoid taking the responsibility for the management of the consultation away from the primary consultant. What seems equally important is the need of the consultant for personal support and for a knowledgeable resource to help monitor what is otherwise a lonely and autonomous role.

Evaluating Consultation

What is the nature of the evidence that supports the utility of organizational consultation, especially of the intervention or change phase? If the reader is thinking of carefully designed research evidence with matched control and experimental groups, then there is little or no support to justify organizational consultation, especially OD.

The reasons for this lack of research should be fairly clear. It is difficult to find a reasonable sample of organizations with similar problems that can be matched and then assigned to experimental and control groups. It would also be difficult to convince those organizations assigned to a control condition to do nothing about their organizational problems until after the end of the research project, as desirable as such a process would be for the researchers. Also, in such an experimental design several consultants would have to be used which would cause variability, making comparability of groups difficult to achieve.

While there are a number of research reports on the impact of consultation upon organizations which we shall review shortly, perhaps the strongest evidence on the effectiveness of consultation is found in internal criteria—the institutionalization of change. The criteria behaviors are agreed upon by the client and consultant and the meeting of these criteria can be regarded as supportive of the utility of the intervention. Since the criteria behaviors were not in evidence prior to the consultant's intervention, the development of these behaviors can be regarded as unlikely to be chance occurrences.

It is recognized that this argument will be unconvincing to skeptical critics, but the published research reports have almost never involved any true control group. Rather, the literature involves detailed case reports involving a single client system or a comparison of several interventions in different client systems or subsystems that compare consequences as a function of differences in the client systems, different consultant orientation or strategies, and so on.

Still another approach is to compare OD interventions that were reported as successes by the consultants with those that were reported as failures. Greiner (1967), for instance, compared 18 different interventions and found three characteristics of successful interventions. These included: (1) strong internal *and* external pressures for organizational change; (2) a gradual involvement of many levels of the organization, including top management, in the process of change; and (3) more shared decision making as against unrelated or delegated decisions.

Bowers (1973) compared four specific interventions—interpersonal process consultation, task process consultation, sensitivity or T-group training, and survey feedback—and the two control conditions of data handback and no treatment on a variety of attitude response measures in 23 organizations. Two of the four interventions—survey feedback and interpersonal process consultation—and the control procedure of data handback led to positive changes on many of the dependent measures. Task process consultation led to no change, while T-group training and no treatment led to negative changes.

Bowers' further analyses of the data strongly suggested that changes in organizational climate in the direction of better communication, shared decision making, and the like were essential for the interventions to produce positive changes and the *only* intervention which changed organizational climate was survey feedback. In other words, when survey feedback was used, the organizational climate could be changed in a positive direction and these charges facilitated the impact of the other interventions. Bowers' results do suggest that the process of organizational change is a complicated one and that we need complex research strategies to measure such changes. Insofar as organizational change is concerned, however, Bowers' results led him to conclude that successful change requires· the redistribution of power in an organization and that this redistribution must occur developmentally, primarily through survey feedback.

In a similar kind of study, Franklin (1976) examined 25 organizations that were involved in some kind of planned change effort and was able to divide these 25 into 11 successful and 14 unsuccessful organizational efforts based upon a variety of attitudinal measures. The same four interventions and two control conditions used in Bowers' study were included. Again, the results are complex and no single dimension distinguished the successful and unsuccessful efforts. However, the successful organizations can be characterized as more open to and able to adjust to change while the successful ones were more stable and maintained status quo in their orientations. The successful groups were more likely to have used internal change agents or consultants who were chosen and trained for this project and they showed more interest in and greater commitment to the change effort. Franklin concludes that the successful groups involved a shared conceptualization of the problem between client and consultant and an agreement as to the appropriate action steps.

In another, similar comparison of 67 published reports of organizational change efforts, Dunn and Swierczek (1977) found support for three of eleven major hypotheses about planned change. The consultation was more successful if the client and consultant had a collaborative relationship, if the consultant adopted a participative orientation rather than one as an expert, and if the consultation strategy involved high levels of participation in the change effort by the client system. On the other hand, eight of their hypotheses received weak or no support, including those concerning differences between profit-making and other organizations, among stable and unstable task environments, internal and external consultants, single- versus multiple-level intervention, and total- versus partial-organizational involvement. The data analysis of Dunn and Swierczek offers rather strong support for the collaborative, participative approach to consultation that has been advocated in this volume.

Similar support is found in the work of Glaser (1977) who compared the impact of four different consultants on four residential treatment centers for disturbed children. His detailed analysis of these consultants led him to conclude that the effective consultant must be open to input from the entire client system and must maintain flexibility about the consultation. The consultant's role needs to be carefully defined, and his or her role as a catalytic agent facilitating two-way communication with the client system needs to be strongly supported by influential persons in that system, hopefully the top executives of the organization and their immediate staff.

That these data do support the possibility of planned organizational change is clear, despite the fact that none of the studies is based on experimental designs. Further, the lessons to be learned from our brief review seem reasonably clear and tend to support the practices we have advocated. For example, successful organizational change depends upon working collaboratively with organizations where there is strong desire for and commitment to change. The change effort needs to involve a broad consistency of the organization, including top management, and the focus of the change should be the climate of the group, particularly the perception of the members about their power in the organization. The change process itself is a slow one and both the client system and the consultant need patience and perseverance in order for the change to occur and be institutionalized.

Most of the research undertaken thus far has concentrated on private, profit-making organizations. We are in the difficult position of having little evidence on the impact of organizational consultation on public and third-sector institutions. The need for attending to this oversight will become increasingly important as these organizations have an ever-increasing impact on our daily lives.

References

Argyris, C. (1969). The incompleteness of social-psychological theory: Examples from small group, cognitive consistency, and attribution research. *American Psychologist* 24: 893–908.

Argyris, C. (1970). *Intervention Theory and Method: A Behavioral Science View.* Reading, Mass.: Addison-Wesley.

Bales, R. F. (1950). *Interaction Process Analysis.* Reading, Mass.: Addison-Wesley.

Bennis, W. G. (1969). *Organization Development: Its Nature, Origins, and Prospects.* Reading, Mass.: Addison-Wesley.

Bion, W. W. (1961). *Experiences in Groups.* London: Tavistock.

Blake, R. R., and J. S. Mouton (1964). *The Managerial Grid.* Houston: Gulf Publishing.

Blake, R. R., and J. S. Mouton (1976). *Consultation.* Reading, Mass.: Addison-Wesley.

Bowen, D. D. (1977). Value dilemmas in organization development. *Journal of Applied Behavioral Science* 13: 545–558.

Bowers, D. G. (1965). Organization control in an insurance company. *Sociometry* 27: 230–44.

Bowers, D. G. (1973). OD techniques and their results in 23 organizations: The Michigan ICL study. *Journal of Applied Behavioral Science* 9: 21–43.

Browne, P. J., C. C. Cotton, and R. T. Golembiewski (1977). Marginality and the OD practitioner. *Journal of Applied Behavioral Science* 13: 493–506.

Burke, W. W., and W. H. Schmidt (1971). Primary target for change: The manager or the organization. In H. A. Hornstein *et al.* (eds.), *Social Intervention: A Behavioral Science Approach.* New York: Free Press, pp. 373–85.

Caplan, G. (1970). *The Theory and Practice of Mental Health Consultation*. New York: Basic Books.

Delbecq, A., and A. van de Ven (1971). A group process model for problem identification and program planning. *Journal of Applied Behavioral Science* 7: 466–91.

Dunn, W. N., and F. W. Swierczek (1977). Planned organizational change: Toward grounded theory. *Journal of Applied Behavioral Science* 13: 135–158.

Eddy, W. B., and R. J. Saunders (1972). Applied behavioral science in urban administrative/political systems. *Public Administration Review* 32:11–16.

Fiedler, F. E. (1967). *A Theory of Leadership Effectiveness*. New York: McGraw-Hill.

Foltz, J. A., J. B. Harvey, and J. McLaughlin (1974). Organization development: A line management function. In J. Adams (ed.), *Theory and Method in Organization Development: An Evolutionary Process*. Arlington, Va.: NTL Institute for Applied Behavioral Science.

Fordyce, J. K., and R. Weil (1971). *Managing with People*. Reading, Mass.: Addison-Wesley.

Franklin, J. L. (1976). Characteristics of successful and unsuccessful organization development. *Journal of Applied Behavioral Science* 12: 471–92.

French, W. L., and C. H. Bell (1973). *Organization Development*. Englewood Cliffs, N. J.: Prentice-Hall.

Freud, S. (1950). Analysis terminable and interminable. In J. Strachey (ed.), *The Collected Papers of Sigmund Freud*. Volume V. London: Hogarth Press. (Originally published in 1937).

Friedlander, F., and L. D. Brown (1974). Organization development. *Annual Review of Psychology* 25: 313–41.

Glaser, E. M. (1977). Facilitation of knowledge utilization by institutions for child development. *Journal of Applied Behavioral Science* 13: 89–109.

Golembiewski, R. T. (1969). Organizational development in public agencies: Perspectives on theory and practice. *Public Administration Review* 29: 367–78.

Goodstein L. D. (1971). Management development and organizational development: A critical difference in focus. *Business Quarterly* 36: 30–37.

Goodstein, L. D. (1972). Organizational development as a model for community consultation. *Hospital and Community Psychiatry* 23: 165–68.

Goodstein, L. D., and R. K. Boyer (1972). Crisis intervention in a municipal agency: A conceptual case history. *Journal of Applied Behavioral Science* 8: 318–40.

Greiner, L. E. (1967). Patterns of organizational change. *Harvard Business Review* 45: 119–28.

Harrison, R. (1972). Understanding your organization's character. *Harvard Business Review* 50: 119–28.

Herzberg, F., B. Mausner, and B. Synderman (1959). *The Motivation to Work.* New York: Wiley.

Kahn, R. L., D. M. Wolfe, R. P. Quin, J. D. Snoek, and R. A. Rosenthal (1964). *Organizational Stress: Studies in Role Conflict and Ambiguity.* New York: Wiley.

Katz, D., and R. L. Kahn (1966). *Social Psychology of Organizations.* New York: Wiley.

Lawrence, P. R., and J. W. Lorsch (1967). *Organization and Environment: Managing Differentiation and Integration.* Boston: Division of Research, Harvard University, Business School.

Levinson, D. J., and B. M. Astrachan (1976). Entry into the mental health centre: A problem in organizational boundary regulation. In E. J. Miller (ed.) *Task and Organization.* London: Wiley, pp. 217–234.

Levitt, T. (1973). *The Third Sector: New Tactics for a Responsive Society.* New York: Amacom Press.

Lewin, K. (1947). Frontiers in group dynamics. *Human Relations* 1: 5–41.

Lewin, K. (1951). *Field theory in social science.* New York: Harper.

Lewin, K., R. Lippitt, and R. K. White (1939). Patterns of aggressive behavior in experimentally developed climates. *Journal of Social Psychology* 10: 271–99.

Likert, R. (1961). *New Patterns of Management.* New York, McGraw-Hill.

Lippitt, R., J. Watson, and B. Westley (1958). *The Dynamics of Planned Change.* New York: Harcourt, Brace, & World.

Lorsch, J. W., and P. R. Lawrence (1972). *Managing Group and Intergroup Relations.* Homewood, Ill.: Irwin-Dorsey.

Maslow, A. H. (1954). *Motivation and Personality.* New York: Harper.

McGill, M. E., and L. M. Wooton (1975). Management in the Third Sector. *Public Administration Review* 35: 444–55.

McGregor, D. (1960). *The Human Side of Enterprise.* New York: McGraw-Hill.

Merrill, F. E. (1957). *Society and Culture.* Englewood Cliffs, N. J.: Prentice-Hall.

Miles, M. B. (1964). On temporary systems. In M. B. Miles (ed.), *Innovation in Education.* New York: Bureau of Publications, Teachers College, Columbia University.

Miller, G. A. (1969). Psychology as a means of promoting human welfare. *American Psychologist* 24: 1063–75.

Miner, J. B. (1963). *The Management of Ineffective Performance.* New York: McGraw-Hill.

Platt, J. (1973). Social traps. *American Psychologist* 28: 641–51.

Rice, A. K. (1958). *Productivity and Social Organization: The Ahmedabad Experiment.* London: Tavistock.

Rice, A. K. (1963). *The Enterprise and the Environment.* London: Tavistock.

Rice, A. K. (1965). *Learning for Leadership.* London: Tavistock.

Rice, A. K. (1969). Individual, group, and intergroup processes. *Human Relations* 22: 565–84.

Roethlisberger, F. J., and W. J. Dickson (1939). *Management and the Worker.* Cambridge, Mass.: Harvard University Press.

Saper, B. (1975). Confessions of a former state hospital superintendent. *Professional Psychology* 6: 367–80.

Sarason, S. B., M. Levine, I. I. Goldenberg, D. L. Cherlin, and E. M. Bennett (1966). *Psychology in Community Settings: Clinical, Educational, Vocational, Social Aspects.* New York: Wiley.

Schein, E. H. (1969). *Process Consultation: Its Role in Organization Development.* Reading, Mass.: Addison-Wesley.

Schmuck, R. A. (1976). Process consultation and organization development. *Professional Psychology* 7: 626–31.

Schmuck, R. A., and M. B. Miles (eds.) (1971). *Organization Development in Schools.* Palo Alto, Ca.: National Press Books.

Schroeder, M. (1974). The shadow consultant. *Journal of Applied Behavioral Science* 10: 579–94.

Stanton, A. H., and M. S. Schwartz (1954). *The Mental Hospital: A Study of Institutional Participation in Psychiatric Illness and Treatment.* New York: Basic Books.

Steele, F. (1973). *Physical Settings and Organization Development.* Reading, Mass.: Addison-Wesley.

Steele, F. (1975). *Consulting for Organizational Change.* Amherst: University of Massachusetts Press.

Stogdill, R. M. (1974). *Handbook of Leadership: A Survey of Theory and Research.* Riverside, N.J.: Free Press.

Trist, E. L., G. W. Higgins, H. Murray, and A. B. Pollack (1963). *Organizational Choice.* London: Tavistock.

van de Vall, M. (1975). Utilization and methodology of applied social research: Four complementary models. *Journal of Applied Behavioral Science* 11: 14–38.

von Bertalanffy, L. (1956). General systems theory. *General Systems* (Yearbook of the Society for the Advancement of General Systems Theory) 1: 1–10.

Walton, R. E. (1969). *Interpersonal Peacemaking: Confrontation and Third Party Consultation.* Reading, Mass.: Addison-Wesley.

Weber, M. (1947). *The Theory of Social and Economic Organization.* New York: Oxford University Press. (Translated from the German by A. M. Henderson and Talcott Parsons.)

Weisbord, M. R. (1976a). Why organization development hasn't worked (so far) on medical centers. *Health Care Mangement Review* 1: 17–28.

Weisbord, M. R. (1976b). Organizational diagnosis: Six places to look for trouble with or without a theory. *Organization and Group Studies* 1: 430–47. Used with permission.

Ziller, R. C. (1973). *The Social Self.* New York: Permagon Press.

Index

Argyris, C., 70, 92, 113–115, 117, 145–147, 156
Astrachan, B. M., 62, 65

Bales, R. F., 69
Bell, C. H., 122–123, 136
Bennett, E. M., 5
Bennis, W. G., 122
Bion, W. W., 64
Blake, R. R., 28, 37, 55–57, 67–68, 110
Boundaries in organizations, 61–62, 65–66
Bowen, D. D., 93–94
Bowers, D. G., 50, 159–160
Boyer, R. K., 69, 78, 84, 97, 155
Brown, L. D., 122–124, 126, 132–133, 139–140
Browne, P. J., 156
Bureaucracy, 8, 22, 109, 132
Burke, W. W., 47, 94

Caplan, G., 23, 55–56, 156
Cherlin, D. L., 5
Cohesion in organizations.
    See Morale.
Communications within organizations, 13, 20, 22, 27, 32, 40–41, 55–56, 68–71, 79, 126
Competition, between organizations, 9

within organizations, 104, 106
Conflict, management of, 13–14,
    84–85, 103, 109, 126, 137, 144
    use of, 108, 156
Consulcube, 28–38, 55–57, 66–69
Cotton, C. C., 156

Delbecq, A., 130
Diagnosis in consultation, 43–46, 63,
    78, 83–84, 87, 95–119, 136
    methods of data collection,
        98–101, 136
    direct observation, 83, 98–99
    interviews, 99–100, 136
    questionnaires, 100–101, 136
    written documents, use of, 99
    resistance to, 96–98, 100
    role of diagnosis in organizational
        change, 113–115
    use of six-box model, 103–113
Dickson, W. J., 69
Dunn, W. N., 160

Eddy, W. B., 9
Effectiveness of organizations, cri-
    teria for, 7, 14, 51–54, 66,
    154
Entry in consultation, 77–94, 96, 116
    contrasting, 86–90
    initial contrast, 5–6, 21, 23–26,
        77–86
    values involved in, 90–94
Evaluation of consultation, 157–161

Fiedler, F. E., 37, 111
Foltz, J. A., 149
Fordyce, J. K., 51–54
Franklin, J. L., 159–160
French, W. L., 122–123, 136
Freud, S., 150
Friedlander, F., 122–124, 126,
    132–133, 139–140

Glaser, E. M., 170
Goals of organizations, 15–17, 32,
    34, 56, 67, 75–76, 98,
    103–105, 127

Goldenberg, I. I., 5
Golembiewski, R., 9–12, 156
Goodstein, L. D., 20, 48, 69, 78, 84,
    97, 140, 155
Greiner, L. E., 158

Harrison, R., 13, 91–92, 100
Harvey, J. B., 149
Herzberg, F., 109
Human service delivery systems, 3,
    5–6, 40–43, 74, 79, 103–105,
    108, 126–133

Internal consultants, 81, 120, 149,
    155–156
Interventions in organizations,
    47–50, 81
    criteria for evaluating, 142–148
    diagnosis as part of intervention,
        95–96, 116–119
    kinds of interventions, 122–141
        process interventions, 133–134
            coaching or counseling,
                133–134
            intergroup development,
                139–141
            survey feedback, 133–136
            team building, 136–139
        technostructural interventions,
            124–133
            job design and enrichment,
                132
            sociotechnical changes,
                126–132
    planning the intervention, 119–120
    terminating the intervention,
        149–150
Institutionalization of change in
    organizations, 142–148

Kahn, R. L., 22, 61, 63
Katz, D., 22, 61, 63

Lawrence, P. R., 73, 139
Leadership, 10–12, 20, 37, 49–50, 55,
    65, 67, 69, 71, 75–76,
    110–111, 118, 136, 138

Levine, M., 5
Levinson, D. J., 62, 65
Levitt, T., 4, 7, 15
Lewin, K., 58, 69, 110, 148
Likert, R., 50
Lippitt, R., 69, 110, 121
Lorsch, J. W., 73, 139

Management development, 48, 123
Management theories, differen-
    tiation-integration, 72-74
  open-systems, 60-64
  Tavistock institute, 64-66
  Theory X and Theory Y, 49-50
Maslow, A. H., 109
McGill, M. E., 15
McGregor, D., 37, 49-50
McLaughlin, J., 149
Mental Health Consultation, 23-27,
    55-56
Merrill, F. E., 15
Miles, M., 5, 136
Miller, G. A., 37
Miner, J. B., 50
Morale in organizations, 2, 34, 56,
    67-68, 117
Mouton, J. S., 28, 37, 55-57, 67-68,
    110

Nominal group procedure, 130-131
Norms in organizations, 10, 31, 34,
    51-54, 56, 62-64, 67-68, 73,
    104, 109, 112-113, 144-147,
    151-152

Objectives of organizations.
    See Goals.
Open-systems theory, 60-64,
    73, 76
Organizational effectiveness, criteria
    of, 7, 8, 51-54
Organizational consultants, effec-
    tiveness of, 157-161
  marginality of, 155-157
  power relationships with clients,
    24, 43-45, 48, 67-68, 80, 82,
    142

resistance to, 96-98, 100, 119-121
role of, 43, 67-68, 70-71, 78, 80,
    83-84, 90-92, 134, 142-143,
    150-157
skills and knowledge required,
    19-22, 58, 68-69, 85-86,
    160-161
termination of, 149-150
Organization Development (OD),
    47-50, 81, 122-124
compared with management
    development, 48, 123

Planned change in organizations.
    See Interventions.
Platt, J., 142
Power issues in organizations, 16,
    34, 48-50, 56, 63-64, 67-68,
    126, 159
Process consultation, 40-46, 50, 55,
    59, 69-71, 80, 88, 97-98,135,
    154
Process issues, 2, 5-6, 41-42, 87-88,
    112, 133-141, 145-146
Process vs. product distinction, 2-4,
    39, 58, 75, 79-80, 122-124
Psychoanalysis, 64-66, 150
Psychopathology in organizations,
    20-21
Public sector organizations, 3-4,
    7-14
  pressures on, 9-10
Purpose of organizations. See Goals.

Research on consultation, 156-161
Rice, A. K., 64, 66, 125
Roethlisberger, F. J., 69
Roles in organizations, 10-11,
    51-54, 62-64, 67, 69, 72-74,
    89

Saper, B., 126
Sareson, S. B., 5
Saunders, R. J., 9
Schein, E. H., 40, 69-71
Schmidt, W. H., 47
Schmuck, R. A., 5, 47

Schroeder, M., 157
Schwartz, M. S., 19
Standards in organizations.
    See Norms.
Stanton, A. H., 19
Steele, F., 83, 150–155
Stogdill, R. M., 110
Structure in organizations, 9, 16, 19,
    22, 62, 65–66, 72–73, 76,
    106–108, 112, 124–133
Survey feedback, 33–34, 100–101,
    134–136, 159
Swierczek, F. W., 160
Symptoms of organizational diffi-
    culties, 1–2, 22, 27, 51–54,
    78, 81–82, 117

Tavistock Institute, 64–66, 99, 125
Team building, 48, 136–141
Technostructural interventions,
    124–133
Third sector organizations, 4, 7,
    14–17

Trist, E. L., 50

Values, of the client, 34–35, 49–50,
    62–64, 73, 101–102, 117,
    144–147
    in the consultation process, 46–54,
    90–94, 114–115, 142,
    153–154, 156
van de Vall, M., 120
van de Ven, A., 130
von Bertelanffy, L., 61

Walton, R. E., 139
Watson, J., 121
Weber, M., 8
Weil, R., 51–54
Weisbord, M. R., 74–75, 103–113,
    135
Westley, B., 121
White, R. K., 69, 110
Wooton, L. M., 15

Ziller, R. C., 173